"Says Who?"

Discovering Worth, Identity, and Purpose in Genesis

Lauren Rice

© 2020 Bill Rice Ranch, Inc. All rights reserved.

Scripture quotations are taken from the *Holy Bible*, King James Version

Printed in the United States of America

No part of this publication may be reproduced, stored in a retrieval system, or transmitted in any form or by any means—electronic, mechanical, photocopy, recording, or any other—without the prior written permission of the publisher. The only exception is brief quotations in printed reviews.

CONTENTS

Chapter 1
"Says Who?": Our Worth as God's Creation

Chapter 2
More Than Many Sparrows: Our Identity & Purpose as God's Creation

Chapter 3
Identity Crisis: Our Identity as God's Children

Chapter 4
"Remember Whose Kid You Are": Our Purpose as God's Children

Chapter 5
"Stay Salty": Our Purpose as Noahs

Chapter 6
Colors of the Rainbow: Finding Purpose in Second Chances

Chapter 7
"That Looks Good on You!": A Biblical Perspective of Self-Esteem

Chapter 8
You Are Not Cast Out: Lessons from Hagar

Chapter 9
"Give Me Your Rice!": Lessons from Abraham

Chapter 10
Don't Tap Out: Lessons from Esau

Chapter 11
Recovering from Christian Agnosticism: Lessons from Jacob

Chapter 12
Choosing Success Over Self-Pity: Lessons from Joseph

All Scripture used is quoted from the King James version of the Bible with emphasis added by the author.

"Take God at His Word about your worth!"

1. "Says Who?": Our Worth as God's Creation

Remember when you and your best friend in elementary school used to play bumper cars at recess? All was hunky-dory until your buddy dove off the swing and landed on both feet in the playground mulch. Then came the challenge.

"C'mon, jump."

You hem-hawed for a bit, scrambling for an excuse to not make the leap. The wind seemed to hit you in the face as you kept swinging and your friend kept staring.

"Aw, you're just chicken."

Your back stiffened and so did your resolve. With two simple words, you could discredit your buddy's accusation.

"Says who?"

In elementary school, the person who made the statement determined the credibility of the statement. If your peers said it, you could prove them wrong. If your teachers said it, their opinion possibly weighed more. And if your parents said it, then it was true!

Says Who?

Whether uttered by children scuffling on a playground or by adults, words are only as credible as their source. If a coward were to call you a chicken, there would not be much reason for you to believe him. You'd think, "Look who's talking!" However, if a Navy Seal were to call you a chicken, you would probably feel challenged to become a braver soul. What a Navy Seal says about bravery carries much more authority than what a draft-dodger says about bravery. *"Says who?" is still a valid question.*

When discussing your worth, the people and influences around you can send mixed messages about what makes you valuable. Whose word do you take for truth? For example, one day your feelings may tell you that your worth is measured in your appearance, and the next day your parents may tell you that it lies in your abilities. As you are scrolling through social media another day, your virtual friends may define your worth by how many likes you receive or followers you get. With so many voices screaming so many different definitions and measurements of your worth, it is no wonder that you may feel slightly confused or even downright depressed about your intrinsic worth as a human being.

According to the American Foundation for Suicide Prevention, 25 million Americans suffer from depression every year, and suicide is the 10th leading cause of death in America today. In addition, *The Daily Wire* recently reported that "youth suicide is in the midst of a precipitous and frightening rise" and that "as of 2016, suicide levels were at 30-year highs."[1] Something is badly wrong, and *The*

---

[1] Shapiro, Ben. "CDC: Youth Suicide Skyrockets 70% Over Last Decade. Here's Why." *The Daily Wire*. Last modified March 20, 2018. https://www.dailywire.com/news/cdc-youth-suicide-skyrockets-70-over-last-decade-ben-shapiro.

Daily Wire suggested that this epidemic is due largely to "a crisis of meaning… heavily linked to a decline in religious observance." [2] While lack of religious observance—attending church, praying etc.—certainly is a problem in this epidemic of hopelessness, the problem is more fundamental than that. The fundamental problem in this alarming trend among young Americans is a misunderstanding of individual human worth!

Our Worth

As humans, we are all tempted to look for our worth in ourselves and our abilities, in our possessions and positions, or in other people and their affirmation of us. One way to know where we are placing our worth is to consider what makes us say "I'm okay" at the end of the day. When the doubts and fears swirl in your brain, with what do you comfort yourself?

"Well, I have those friends. They've accepted me, so I'm okay."

"I'm okay because I finally have that position I've worked so hard for at work!"

"At least I can still do that really well, so I'm okay."

"Finally, I've made it here. Now I'm okay."

"They say I still have my good looks. I guess I'm okay."

"Remember, I won that medal last weekend at the race, so I'm okay."

Whatever subdues the fears for the moment is the person, place, or thing that we believe defines our worth. The problem is that one day those affirmations will no longer be enough. A day will come when the doubts or the fears are louder than the looks, or the abilities, or the other people affirming us.

In order to discover the cure to this epidemic of hopelessness, we must discover the truth about our worth. What makes our lives worthwhile in the first place? What better place to start searching for the answer to this most basic question than Genesis, the book of beginnings!

First, we must answer the basic question: *Who gets to create our identities and determine our worth?*

▶ READ

Genesis 1:1-3, 6-7, 9, 14, 20, 24

> In the beginning **God created** the heaven and the earth.
> And the earth was without form, and void; and darkness was upon the face of the deep. And the Spirit of God moved upon the face of the waters.
> **And God said,** Let there be light: **and there was light**.
>
> **And God said,** Let there be a firmament in the midst of the waters, and let it divide the waters from the waters.

---

[2] Ibd.

And **God made** the firmament, and divided the waters which were under the firmament from the waters which were above the firmament: **and it was so**.

And God said, Let the waters under the heaven be gathered together unto one place, and let the dry land appear: **and it was so.**

And God said, Let there be lights in the firmament of the heaven to divide the day from the night; and let them be for signs, and for seasons, and for days, and years:

And God said, Let the waters bring forth abundantly the moving creature that hath life, and fowl that may fly above the earth in the open firmament of heaven.

And God said, Let the earth bring forth the living creature after his kind, cattle, and creeping thing, and beast of the earth after his kind: **and it was so.**

The Bible often repeats key words for emphasis, and the word pattern in these verses clues us into the source of our worth. The pattern is *And God said...and it was so*. As these verses introduce the Author and main Character of the Bible, they also describe His first actions. The Author and main Character, God, created light, the sky, the galaxies and the planets within them. God spoke the oceans, the sea creatures, and all kinds of land animals into existence. The Hebrew word translated "create" in Genesis 1:1 is *bara*, meaning to create or produce out of new conditions or circumstances. In other words, God produced all of that out of nothing! From the very beginning, God is established as the Ultimate Authority of the Universe. Yet even more astounding than God's creating the earth and the animals out of nothing is the way in which God decided to create the first human being ever.

▶ READ

Genesis 2:7

> **And the LORD God formed man** of the dust of the ground, and breathed into his nostrils the breath of life; **and man became a living soul**.

In this verse, the pattern is not, And God said....and it was so. The Bible says that *God formed...and man became!* The Hebrew word translated "form" in this verse is *yatsar*, a word that carries the idea of fashioning or producing with a plan, design, or purpose in mind. In the same way that a potter forms the clay into a particular shape to serve a particular purpose, the God of the Universe bent down to form humankind for a special purpose. Not only did God form him, but God breathed the breath of life into his nostrils. This special type of creation was not used only in the case of the first man, Adam. This special type of creation is the way God chose to create *you*—with a plan, design, and purpose. In these next verses, listen to God's heart for you:

> ### ▶ READ
>
> Jeremiah 1:5
>> Before **I formed thee** in the belly **I knew thee**; and before thou camest forth out of the womb I sanctified thee, and I ordained thee a prophet unto the nations.
>
> Psalm 139:13-16
>> For thou hast possessed my reins: thou hast covered me in my mother's womb.
>> I will praise thee; for I am fearfully and wonderfully made: marvelous are thy works; and that my soul knoweth right well.
>> My substance was not hid from thee, when I was made in secret, and curiously wrought in the lowest parts of the earth.
>> Thine eyes did see my substance, yet being unperfect; and in thy book all my members were written, which in continuance were fashioned, when as yet there was none of them.

When we open the book of Jeremiah, we meet a tepid man, not a great prophet. When God commissioned Jeremiah, He prefaced it with the affirmation of Jeremiah's worth. That affirmation did not include a "you can do it" pep talk. God did not list Jeremiah's good looks and many abilities and social status in His affirmation of Jeremiah's worth. The affirmation we find in verse five is very simply, "God created you and God knew you." That's it! The fact that God created and knew Jeremiah before his birth affirms Jeremiah's worth.

This truth is reaffirmed in Psalm 139. Did you catch those key words in Psalm 139—*possessed, made, fashioned*? Just for a moment, meditate on the truth that God possessed you before you were put together, and He protected you in your mother's womb. He formed you in your mother's belly just the way he wanted you to be. Before your mother even realized you existed, God knew you to your very core! Every intricate detail about you God knows by heart because He created each of those details! At the end of your creation, God sat back, looked at you, and said, *it is very good*.

God's Creation

Friend, you have intrinsic worth. "Says who?" you may ask. From these verses, the answer is evident! Society doesn't get to determine your worth because society didn't form you in your mother's belly. In fact, your mother doesn't get to determine your worth because it wasn't her responsibility to form you with her own hands. Your friends don't get to determine your worth, because they didn't know you before you were born, and they couldn't possibly understand your intricacies like God does. Not only do other people not have the right to define your worth, but *you* don't even have the right to define your worth. Remember—you didn't form you! God did. It only makes logical sense that the Creator of your life gets to determine the worth of your life. Because your worth is settled in heaven, nothing you do and no person you know can take that away from you. Take God at His Word about your worth!

The first step to understanding your worth is realizing who says you have worth. On what authority do you know that your life has worth? In the end, even if everything is stripped from you, your life will still have worth because God created it. Your worth will still be intact no matter your appearance, abilities, or aptitudes. You will always be worth infinity and beyond. "Says who?" you ask.

Says God!

▶ Time to think!

WHAT ARE SOME PLACES, PEOPLE, OR THINGS UPON WHICH YOU HAVE BEEN TEMPTED TO BASE YOUR WORTH?

___

___

___

WHAT WAS GOD'S AFFIRMATION OF JEREMIAH'S WORTH IN CHAPTER ONE?

___

___

___

WHAT ARE SOME KEY WORDS FOUND IN PSALM 139?

_____

_____

_____

WHO HAS THE RIGHT TO DEFINE YOUR WORTH AND WHY?

_____

_____

_____

NOTES

"Only God-worship will satisfy our greatest longing
and fill our deepest emptiness!"

2 More Than Many Sparrows:
Our Identity & Purpose as God's Creation

As a child, and now as a more grown-up child, one of my favorite outings was going to the zoo. I have many fond memories of visiting the Nashville Zoo with my Grandmom, my younger brothers, and my cousins on a sweltering summer day. One of my favorite exhibits was the goat pen! Yes, the goat pen. The reason I loved the goat pen so much was that we were allowed to go inside to pet and feed the goats. Every chance I got to interact with furry creatures, I took it. Ever since I can remember, I've always wanted to stop and pet any dog I saw walking with its person on the street or adopt yet another pet even though I already had enough, according to my parents. To this day, I love to see the deer frolic in the field outside my house.

How about you? Whether or not you derive as much joy from animals as I do, we can certainly agree that animals are fascinating creations. They instinctively know what to do in order to survive, and they have fun while they are doing it! I remember one spring morning, I stared out into my green and blooming front yard and just marveled at these little animals. I watched the scurrying squirrels hoard nuts and the brilliant hummingbirds hovering over the flower buds and wondered why I couldn't be like them. Why couldn't my purpose be as simple as survival, and why couldn't I just instinctively know what to do in order to accomplish that purpose? What made me so different than the squirrel in my front yard?

When you and I consider our purpose, we long for something beyond survival. Our greatest desire is not to strive all our days for the sole purpose of survival. We want to accomplish more than just survive—we want to thrive! Our hearts whisper that there must be more to life than collecting nuts for winter ease.

Our Unique Identity

In the last chapter, we learned where our intrinsic worth comes from. We are priceless creations of God that cannot be replicated or replaced. In this chapter, we will discover *how our God-established identity makes us unique* from the rest of creation. Our identity as creations of God is way more profound than we often realize! We are not creations of God in the same way that your precious pet is a creation of God. We are not the same type of creation as the mighty tree that towers in the backyard nor the same as the rose bushes that bloom in the front yard. God put something in humans that He did not put into animals or plants or anything else He created. Let's take a look:

READ

Genesis 1:26-27

And God said, Let us make man in our image, after our likeness: and let them have dominion over the fish of the sea, and over the fowl of the air, and over the cattle, and over all the earth, and over every creeping thing that creepeth upon the earth.

So God created man in his own image, in the image of God created he him; male and female created he them.

Matthew 10:29-31

Are not two sparrows sold for a farthing? and one of them shall not fall on the ground without your Father.

But the very hairs of your head are all numbered.

Fear ye not therefore, ye are of more value than many sparrows.

Contrary to our belief at times, God never misses one thing that happens here on earth. When the smallest sparrow falls to the ground, God notices. And God tells us in Matthew 10 that we are worth more than many sparrows! The difference between us and the sparrows is the image of God Himself! Our identity as a creation of God is that of an image bearer. That phrase "in the image of God" bears weight because your purpose hinges on what that phrase means. In Genesis 1:26, the Hebrew word *tselem* that is translated "image" means "resemblance." This created-by-God truth just keeps getting more exciting, doesn't it? *The fact that we bear God's image means that our purpose as His creation is to resemble God in some way.* Of course, this doesn't mean we are to resemble God in our appearance because no one knows what God looks like. However, as image-bearers, we bear some characteristics that are small glimpses of what God Himself is like. In sum, being an image-bearer gives us the purpose of reflecting God's character to the world around us. In everything we do, we are to give the world a glimpse, though an imperfect one, of what God is like! What a purpose!

Language

How did God create the Universe in six literal days? Apart from the creation of man, God spoke it into existence. God used words, *language*. How does God communicate with us today? God communicates with us through the Bible, *His written Word*.

Words—whether they be spoken or written— are essential for communication. And this is one way that we are distinct from the rest of creation. Unlike the plants and animals, we have the God-like characteristic of language. Through language, we have the opportunity to communicate clearly and to form deep relationships with others. Specifically, God gave us the gift of language so that we could communicate with *Him* and develop a personal relationship with *Him*. The thought that the God of the Universe wants to be our personal Father and Friend is mind-blowing.

As image-bearers, part of our purpose is communicating with God personally and speaking His truth to the world through the God-given characteristic of language.

Creativity

Not only do we possess the God-like characteristic of language, but we also have the God-like characteristic of creativity! As the astounding Creator of the entire amazing Universe, God is the Ultimate Creative Being. The colors, layers, diversity, and unique beauty of this planet alone is overwhelming, but to think that One Being imagined it all and created it is incredible. God's creation has captivated people for centuries. Some people have attempted to capture God's creation on canvas. Others have sought to express the inspiration and awe they feel from creation through powerful notes and lyrics on page. Many have captured the grandeur of creation through a camera lens or described it for others on pen and paper.

Inspired by the Ultimate Creator, people are little creators, using the tools God has given to make new and beautiful things. As image-bearers, we all have some measure of creativity. While our areas of creativity will vary from art to writing, from fashion to music, from interior design to cooking, we share the same purpose. Our purpose as image-bearers is to use our creations to draw eyes back to our Creator.

Will & Emotions

Have you ever wished you could just banish your emotions for a day? Sometimes emotions cloud our judgment and influence our decisions. While emotions can often get in the way, life would be completely boring without them. Without emotions, we would be incomplete shells of human beings.

Although we often resent emotions, the part of us that feels deep emotion is a God-like characteristic. Many of the emotions we have felt, God Himself has felt, except without sin. When He was on earth, Jesus expressed emotions that we are well-acquainted with. For example, Luke 10:21 says that *"Jesus rejoiced* in spirit" and thanked the Father after sharing a parable with a crowd. In Matthew 14:14, Jesus expressed feelings for the crowds that thronged him. He *"was moved with compassion toward them*, and he healed their sick." In John 11:35, *Jesus wept* over the death of his friend Lazarus. As the Old Testament prophet foretold in Isaiah 53:3, Jesus was "a man of sorrows and acquainted with grief." Jesus also displayed emotions of anger over sin in John 2:15, and the Bible likewise commands us to be angry at sin in Deuteronomy 6:13-15. Several passages in John use the phrase *"Jesus loved"* in relation to His disciples, his mother, and his brethren. These passages and many others throughout the Bible indicate that emotions are part of how God expresses Himself to His creation. Although God could have chosen to create us as cold, calculating robots and coerced us to "love" Him, He chose to create us as free agents, image-bearers, capable of choosing to love Him. This combination of will and emotions is unique to the human creation. Animals do not have the same capacity to make decisions and express emotions. Even a dog can be coerced to love someone if he is given enough treats! In contrast with our beloved pets, we have the ability to choose God and love God, no treats attached!

While our emotions can be used to guide us away from God, they are intended to guide us toward Him. When we channel our God-given emotions (like Jesus did!) rather than let them control us, we can use our emotions to reflect God's character to the world. In the following verses, we see the characteristics of language, creativity, and emotions on display:

▶ READ

Genesis 2:15-24

And the LORD God took the man, and put him into the garden of Eden to dress it and to keep it.

And the LORD God commanded the man, saying, Of every tree of the garden thou mayest freely eat:

But of the tree of the knowledge of good and evil, thou shalt not eat of it: for in the day that thou eatest thereof thou shalt surely die. [Will]

And the LORD God said, It is not good that the man should be alone; I will make him an help meet for him.

And out of the ground the LORD God formed every beast of the field, and every fowl of the air; and brought them unto Adam to see what he would call them: and whatsoever Adam called every living creature, that was the name thereof.

And **Adam gave names** [Language/Creativity] to all cattle, and to the fowl of the air, and to every beast of the field; but for Adam there was not found an help meet for him.

And the LORD God caused a deep sleep to fall upon Adam, and he slept: and he took one of his ribs, and closed up the flesh instead thereof;

And the rib, which the LORD God had taken from man, made he a woman, and brought her unto the man.

And Adam said [Language], This is now bone of my bones, and flesh of my flesh: she shall be called Woman, because she was taken out of Man.

Therefore, **shall a man leave** his father and his mother, and **shall cleave unto his wife**: and they shall be one flesh. [Will/Emotions]

From these verses, we see three of the God-like characteristics—language, creativity, and will and emotions. In the act of naming the animals, Adam expressed both language and creativity. How would you like to be responsible to name every species of animal on earth? I don't know about you, but I certainly never would have the creativity to come up with all those names. Adam was given an opportunity to use his will and emotions when God gave Adam a choice between obeying God or eating of the forbidden tree. Adam's will and emotions were certainly involved when he met Eve for the first time!

So much can be gleaned from these verses, but we see that God gave humankind the ability to communicate, create, and display deep-felt emotion as God does. And God created Adam and Eve with each of these characteristics for the purpose of having a personal relationship with Him. Like the first man and woman, we can do something that the goats at the zoo can't do. We are image-bearers with the ability to know God and reflect Him to the world around us!

▶ Time to think!

WHAT MAKES US DIFFERENT FROM THE REST OF CREATION?

_____

_____

_____

WHAT IS OUR PURPOSE AS IMAGE-BEARERS?

_____

_____

_____

WHAT ARE SOME SPECIFIC GOD-GIVEN CHARACTERISTICS THAT WE SHOULD USE TO REFLECT GOD TO THE WORLD AROUND US?

_____

_____

_____

Our Unique Purpose

With this great identity as image-bearers comes an equally great purpose and responsibility. Since God was good enough to give us the unique privilege of reflecting Him to the world, we are not to waste our God-given characteristics in pursuit of our own selfish desires. Scripture clearly paints the picture that our ultimate purpose as image-bearers is to please and glorify God.

▶ READ

Isaiah 43:7
> Even every **one** that is called by my name: for **I have created him for my glory,** I have formed him; yea, I have made him.

Psalm 147:11
> **The LORD taketh pleasure in them that fear him**, in those that hope in his mercy.

Luke 2:13-14, 20a
> And suddenly there was with the angel a multitude of the heavenly host praising God, and saying,
> **Glory to God in the highest**, and on earth peace, good will toward men.
>
> And the shepherds returned, **glorifying and praising God.**

1 Corinthians 6:20b
> Therefore **glorify** God in your body, and in your spirit, which are God's.

1 Peter 4:11b
> …If any man minister, let him do it as of the ability which God giveth: **that God in all things may be glorified.**

Colossians 1:16-17
> For by **him** were all things created, that are in heaven, and that are in earth, visible and invisible, whether they be thrones, or dominions, or principalities, or powers: **all things were created by him, and for him.**
> And he is before all things, and by him all things consist.

Romans 1:21
> Because that, when they knew God, **they glorified him not as God,** neither were thankful; but became vain in their imaginations, and their foolish heart was darkened.

Glorify God

From the Old Testament to the New, God takes pleasure in those who glorify Him. Isaiah states that we were created for God's glory. The sweet psalmist sang that God is pleased when we fear Him. When the angles burst onto the scene with the news of Christ's birth, they sang "glory to God in the highest." What did the shepherds do when they heard the angel's song? They also glorified God! During his life on earth, Christ's mission was to glorify the Father.

If Christ was born to glorify God, why shouldn't we glorify God as well? Our life purpose, our responsibility as image bearers, is wrapped up in the four words found in Colossians 1:16-17, "*by Him and for Him.*" Without Jesus, the Creator, we would have no life. And without glorifying Him, we cannot lead fulfilling lives.

In our fallen human state, we may balk at this idea of giving God the credit and long to glorify ourselves instead. That is what the people in Romans 1:21 did. The sin against which we are so strongly admonished in Romans 1 is not primarily fornication or idolatry, but it is the failure to glorify God and the choice to glorify self instead. Ironically, when we humans set out to glorify ourselves instead of God, we can never do enough or be enough to satisfy ourselves.

This insatiable desire for fulfillment testifies to the fact that our hearts were not made to be filled with ourselves and our glory. We were made for some higher purpose—to glorify and please God. God created us so that only God-worship will satisfy our greatest longing and fill our deepest emptiness.

God Doesn't Need Us

While we reap the benefits of a fulfilled and purposeful life from glorying Him, God doesn't need our lives or our worship for fulfillment or satisfaction! In truth, God is not missing out on anything when we do not choose to glorify Him. Why, then, has God created our hearts, so that only God-worship will satisfy us? The answer is simply, God wants us!

In contrast to God, most of our closest loved ones need us to some extent. They need our attention or affection. Our abilities or personalities balance them out. Giving them what they need and getting from them what we need is satisfying and it is the way God made human relationships to be.

However, God didn't create us because He needs us. He doesn't need our attention or affection. He doesn't need our abilities or personalities (He *gave* them to us!). No, God doesn't need us one iota. God wants us. Let that sink in: *God wants you*. When we consider God's mind-blowing love for us and desire to be with us, we should be jumping at the chance to glorify and please Him with our lives.

▶ **Time to think!**

AS IMAGE-BEARERS, WHAT IS OUR PRIMARY PURPOSE AND RESPONSIBILITY?

_____

_____

_____

Now, let's make our purpose practical! How can we best reflect God's character and glorify God before others? Well, as I John 4:16 tells us, God is love. We've seen His love for us already in the way that He created us to be relational beings with Him. If God is love, then we ought to reflect that characteristic to the world around us.

What Glorifying God Looks Like

The most basic way that we can fulfill our purpose as image-bearers is through love. In Matthew 22, after seeing Jesus confound a group of Sadducees with His wisdom, a certain Pharisee approached Jesus about how to best glorify God. As a Pharisee, this man was well-learned in the art of "pleasing God," or rather keeping the law in hopes of earning favor with God. In verse 36, the Pharisee asked, "Master, which is the great commandment in the law?"

Jesus replied in verses 37-39, "*Thou shalt love the Lord thy God with all thy heart, and with all thy soul, and with all thy mind. This is the first and great commandment. And the second is like unto it, Thou shalt love thy neighbor as thyself. On these two commandments hang all the law and the prophets.*"

According to Jesus, the greatest way to glorify God is to love God and others. Why would God classify loving others as the greatest commandment second only to loving God Himself? In John 15:11-14, Jesus told his disciples, "*These things have I spoken unto you, that my joy might remain in you, and that your joy might be full. This is my commandment, That ye love one another, <u>as I have loved you</u>. Greater love hath no man than this, that a man lay down his life for his friends. Ye are my friends, if ye do whatsoever I command you.*" Jesus said that we best glorify and reflect God to the world when we love others because God Himself is love. Jesus proved His love for us when He came to earth to lay down His life for us. We reflect Jesus' love when we follow His command to love others that same way.

What Love Looks Like

Reflecting God's selfless and sacrificial love is a tall order for us as image-bearers! How can we show this kind of love? Again, Jesus is our example, showing us what loving others looks like in a practical, everyday way. In John 13, Jesus sat in the upper room with His disciples over Passover, and "*having loved his own which were in the world … He riseth from supper, and laid aside his garments; and took a towel, and girded himself*" (v. 1, 4). In the space of four verses, the verbs "love" and "riseth" appear in direct relation to each other.

Because Jesus loved his own, He proceeded to serve them…by washing their feet! In the disciples' culture, foot-washing was a humbling act of service. Just to make sure the disciples connected the dots, Jesus said, "*Know ye what I have done to you? Ye call me Master and Lord: and ye say well; for so I am. If I then, your Lord and Master, have washed your feet; ye also ought to wash one another's feet. For I have given you an example, that ye should do as I have done to you*" (v. 12-15). As the disciples learned from Jesus that night, we should realize love and serving others go hand in hand. Christ's example shows us over and over again that the best way to glorify God is to serve others! Consider what these passages say about our relation to others:

▶ **READ**

Luke 6:31-36

And as ye would that men should do to you, do ye also to them likewise.
For if ye love them which love you, what thank have ye? For sinners also love those that love them.
And if ye do good to them which do good to you, what thank have ye? For sinners also do even the same.

And if ye lend to them of whom ye hope to receive, what thank have ye? For sinners also lend to sinners, to receive as much again.
But **love ye your enemies**, and **do good**, and **lend, hoping for nothing again**; and your reward shall be great, **and ye shall be the children of the Highest**: for he is kind unto the unthankful and to the evil.
Be ye therefore merciful, as your Father also is merciful.

Galatians 5:13-14
For, brethren, ye have been called to liberty; only use not liberty for an occasion to the flesh, but **by love serve one another**.
For all the law is fulfilled in one word, even in this; Thou shalt love thy neighbor as thyself.

Galatians 6:2
Bear ye one another's burdens, and so fulfill the law of Christ.

Ephesians 4:2
With all lowliness and meekness, with longsuffering, **forbearing one another in love**;

I John 4:11-12, 20-21
Beloved, if God so loved us, we ought also to love one another.
No man hath seen God at any time. If we love one another, God dwelleth in us, and his love is perfected in us.

If a man say, I love God, and hateth his brother, he is a liar: for he that loveth not his brother whom he hath seen, how can he love God whom he hath not seen?
And this commandment have we from him, That **he who loveth God love his brother also.**

Love Looks Like Serving

The glory of God is seen when we love our enemies, when we give without expecting anything in return, when we serve those who cannot return the favor, and when we show mercy. When we do these things, we are identifying ourselves as "children of the Highest." As the other passages indicate, God-like love includes burden-bearing and longsuffering. In short, all of these verses indicate that loving others practically translates into serving others. Serving others is really just an extension of loving and glorifying God.

While serving others may sound like

an intimidating job, it starts with the smallest aspects of life. Serving may not be demonstrated through foot-washing in our culture today, but it may be shown through inviting people into our home and showing hospitality. Serving can be as simple as giving a smile to a stranger, giving someone else the extra portion of dessert, or offering to help someone with a project on Saturday. Serving may be simply initiating a conversation with someone at church, inviting someone to sit with you in Sunday school, or asking if there is a place of service that you can help fill at church.

As we saw from the previous verses, serving others certainly includes kindness, forgiveness, and doing right by others. You don't have to be a Christian celebrity to influence people and change your world. There are people that only you can reach because of your unique makeup, personality, ability, and position. You may never realize the scope of your influence until you reach heaven.

It's A Wonderful Life

One Christmas tradition in my home is cozying up on the couch while watching the Frank Capra film, *It's A Wonderful Life*. Whether you find the story enjoyable or bizarre, the takeaway from the story is, at its root, a biblical principle. Set in the 1930s, the story follows the life of George Bailey, a man who grows up in the small town of Bedford Falls with dreams of traveling the world and doing what he calls "big things." However, when his generous father dies suddenly, George is saddled with his father's company, Bailey Brothers' Building and Loan. George faces a decision: do something for himself or continue to serve others in the community.

From saving his little brother's life when they were children to sparing his former employer from jail, George has spent himself for other people. After a brief internal struggle, George takes over the Building and Loan. As the new owner of the Building and Loan, George gives people the opportunity to build and own their own homes without having to grovel to the town's richest and cruelest man, Mr. Potter. Then, one fateful Christmas Eve, George's employee, Uncle Billy, accidentally misplaces $8,000! Rather than depositing it in the bank as he intended, Uncle Billy leaves it in Mr. Potter's lap! Uncle Billy's mistake puts George in a difficult position—facing bankruptcy and possibly jail. Frustrated with what he never accomplished and bewildered by the thought of Bedford Falls falling into the hands of Mr. Potter despite a lifetime of efforts, George thinks that everyone he loves would be better off without him.

Just as he is contemplating jumping off a bridge, an angel is summoned by the prayers of George's loved ones. This peculiar angel leaps into the raging river below, knowing that George will jump in to save him. After George rescues the angel from the river, he opens up to the angel about his problems. When George declares that he wishes he'd never been born, the angel gives him a unique gift—the chance to see what life would be like without George Bailey in it!

What George discovers is that he actually had *a wonderful life* and that it would be a shame to throw it away. In the end, when George is returned to his normal life, all the friends he had helped over the years pitch in to come up with the money Uncle Billy had lost. The movie closes with George Bailey surrounded by his family and friends and a note that the angel left: "No one is a failure who has friends." Another way to say it is: No one is a failure who serves others; who *is* a friend. As this story illustrates, one little life can make a huge difference in the world when it is given to loving and serving others.

▶ Time to think!

AS IMAGE-BEARERS, WHAT IS THE BEST WAY WE CAN GLORIFY GOD?

_____

_____

_____

WHO ARE SOME SPECIFIC PEOPLE THAT YOU CAN REACH OUT TO AND SERVE?

_____

_____

_____

HOW CAN YOU BE PROACTIVE ABOUT SERVING THOSE AROUND YOU (I.E. SPECIFIC ACTIONS YOU CAN TAKE)?

_____

_____

_____

NOTES

"Yes, you are still in this dirty, scary, sin-cursed world, but remember who you are!"

3 Identity Crisis: Our Identity as God's Children

One bright Sunday morning, a young woman named Samantha walked into her comfortable and familiar Sunday school class, only to be greeted by someone not-so-familiar. In Samantha's normal Sunday school seat sat a new young woman with long wavy locks, big eyes that seemed to sparkle, and an outfit that screamed affluence. Samantha swallowed hard before forcing herself to approach the young woman and paste on a smile.

"Hello, my name is Samantha. I don't think I've met you before," she began after clearing her throat.

"Oh, hi! I'm Kara," the woman answered with a sparkling white smile. "I just moved here for work."

"Ok, cool! What do you do?" Samantha asked through a less-than-sparkling smile. Kara seemed to light up even more as she explained. "Oh, I'm an ambassador for one of the largest and fastest-growing wellness companies in the country right now. I sell products and coach people about their health and exercise goals."

"Wow!" exclaimed Samantha, blinking. "So… how do you like it?"

"I'm so passionate about health and exercise so I really love what I do. You know, getting to meet new people all the time and train them and help them achieve their health goals—it's super rewarding! Personally, I prefer running as my favorite exercise. I'm currently training for my first half-marathon!"

Samantha stood there smiling as a thousand thoughts raced through her brain. *She's passionate about her job. And she's obviously successful too, or else she wouldn't be wearing such an expensive looking, gorgeous outfit. A half-marathon?! I can hardly puff my way through a 5K! In fact, I've never actually placed in a 5K. And look at that hair. I worked all morning to try to get mine to look like that, but mine still looks flat and lifeless. Oh well.*

Soon Samantha snapped back to the present when Kara asked, "So, what do you do?"

A lump formed in Samantha's throat as she carefully mulled over the words she would say. *How do I make my life sound significant after all that? I'm not a successful business woman or a marathon runner!*

"Oh . . . well, I'm just a college student right now," she offered with a nervous laugh.

"Ok, nice. What are you studying?"

"Yeah, I'm a . . . I'm a Bible major. I hope to use it, you know, in ministry."

"That's neat," Kara replied with a polite smile and nod.

Samantha's eyes wandered around the room looking for the next direction to point the conversation, but her thoughts were interrupted when the teacher welcomed the class. Offering a tepid smile and polite laugh, Samantha nodded goodbye to Kara and took a seat in the row behind her normal Sunday school seat.

The Comparison Trap

Perhaps you can relate to Samantha's awkward Sunday morning conversation with the "new person." While this conversation was quite exaggerated, surely we have all had a conversation that *sounded* like this to us. Even when we are not seeking to compare ourselves with others, sometimes comparison is handed to us on a silver platter. In a blink, we have fallen into the comparison trap that causes us to question our own identities!

Like Samantha and Kara in our story, we humans are very identity oriented. We all like to feel a part of a group or claim a title that makes us feel secure and special. The identity struggle may look different for each of us. We each may seek for it in very different places, but we all seek to put our identity somewhere. Some seek to put their identity in college degrees, good grades, or solid careers. Others find identity in their accomplishments or talents. Still others place their identity in a relationship status, friendship, or possessions. The problem arises when that group disowns them, the place changes, the relationship dies, or the thing fades away. Then they experience what is called an identity crisis.

The First Identity Crisis

Well, it didn't take long for humans to struggle with their identity. Genesis chapter three describes humankind's first-ever identity crisis! God's crowning creations, Adam and Eve, enjoyed a perfect life surrounded by God's beautiful and flawless creation. They enjoyed daily communication and a close friendship with God Himself. They knew who they were—God's image bearers—and they knew their worth. Life was perfect! The only limit to their reign in the perfect garden of Eden was God's command not to eat from the tree of the knowledge of good and evil.

As was His plan from the beginning of creation, God wanted Adam and Eve to have a relationship with Him, but He wanted them to choose to enter that relationship. God didn't create robots, or even a dog, to be his companion. God wanted genuine love and devotion from His crowning creation, humankind!

Then entered Satan—the fallen angel who would not accept his purpose as a creation and worshipper of God. Just as Satan couldn't abide living out God's purpose for his life, neither could he stand the thought of Adam and Eve sweetly and securely living out their God-given identity and purpose. In the form of a serpent, Satan posed the same question to Eve that he poses to you and me today: "*Hath God said?*" (Genesis 3:1). Satan planted a seed of doubt about God's Word and character, suggesting that Eve could and should create her own identity. Satan insisted that if she ate the fruit, she would "*be as gods*" (Genesis 3:5). She watered that seed of doubt when she took the forbidden fruit in hand and perhaps rolled it around in her palm, admiring its pretty skin. Then she wanted what Satan had to offer—the chance to be as wise and all-knowing as God—and she ate the fruit. She chose to trade her perfect relationship with the God of the universe for a piece of fruit.

When Eve fell for Satan's trick in the garden and Adam joined her in the choice to reject God's way, sin entered the world. No longer were Adam and Eve simply defined as crowning creations and image-bearers of God. They were defined by that original and devastating act of sin—choosing pride over peace with God. Since that day, every person has been born stamped with the image of God on them, but also stamped with Satan's mark of sin.

▶ READ

Genesis 3:1-7

> Now the serpent was more subtle than any beast of the field which the LORD God had made. And he said unto the woman, Yea, **hath God said,** Ye shall not eat of every tree of the garden?
> And the woman said unto the serpent, We may eat of the fruit of the trees of the garden:
> But of the fruit of the tree which is in the midst of the garden, God hath said, Ye shall not eat of it, neither shall ye touch it, lest ye die.
> And the serpent said unto the woman, Ye shall not surely die:
> For God doth know that in the day ye eat thereof, then your eyes shall be opened, **and ye shall be as gods**, knowing good and evil.
> And when the woman saw that the tree was good for food, and that it was pleasant to the eyes, and a tree to be desired to make one wise, she took of the fruit thereof, and did eat, and gave also unto her husband with her and he did eat.
> And the eyes of them both were opened, and they knew that they were naked; and they sewed fig leaves together, and made themselves aprons.

Genesis 4

Isaiah 64:6

> But **we are all as an unclean thing**, and all our righteousnesses are as filthy rags; and we all do fade as a leaf; and our iniquities, like the wind, have taken us away.

Romans 3:10-23

> As it is written, There is none righteous, no, not one:
> There is none that understandeth, there is none that seeketh after God.
> They are all gone out of the way, they are together become unprofitable; there is none that doeth good, no, not one.
> Their throat is an open sepulchre; with their tongues they have used deceit; the poison of asps is under their lips:
> Whose mouth is full of cursing and bitterness:
> Their feet are swift to shed blood:

Destruction and misery are in their ways:
And the way of peace have they not known:
There is no fear of God before their eyes.
Now we know that what things soever the law saith, it saith to them who are under the law: that every mouth may be stopped, and **all the world may become guilty before God**.
Therefore by the deeds of the law there shall no flesh be justified in his sight: for by the law is the knowledge of sin.
But now the righteousness of God without the law is manifested, being witnessed by the law and the prophets;
Even the righteousness of God which is by faith of Jesus Christ unto all and upon all them that believe: for there is no difference.
For **all have sinned**, and come short of the glory of God;

Romans 5:12
Wherefore as by one man sin entered the world, and death by sin; and so death passed upon all men, for that **all have sinned.**

Damaged Goods

In Genesis chapter four, within just one generation, the first murderer, Cain, took his own brother's life. Also in Genesis chapter four, we are also introduced to Lamech, a descendent of Cain who followed in his forefather's murderous footsteps. This sin mark is inescapable. As Romans 3 describes it, this sin problem is like snake venom coursing through our veins.

The evidence is clear: We are damaged goods. Every single human on earth is a precious creation of God, but not everyone is a child of God. At our core, we are sinners. That is who we are. That is our identity. In our sinful state, we are literally incapable of having a relationship with a holy God.

Romans three explains that the law condemns us and that no amount of law keeping could save us. All of our good works are like filthy rags to a holy God (Isaiah 64:6) because even those good deeds come from a person who is a sinner at his core. No matter how hard we may try, we will always fall short of God's standard for heaven—absolute perfection (Romans 3:23). Some of us humans display our sinful core in horrible ways, like Cain and Lamech did in Genesis chapter four. Others, like Abel, perform good works in spite of their sinful core. Yet no amount of good works can change who we are at our core: sinners. We could never do enough good to change our identity and make ourselves right with a holy God. As grim as our sin situation is, God didn't leave us in our identity crisis.

> **READ**

Romans 5:6-10

> **For when we were yet without strength**, in due time **Christ died for the ungodly**.
> For scarcely for a righteous man will one die: yet peradventure for a good man some would even dare to die.
> **But** God commendeth his love toward us, in that, **while we were yet sinners**, Christ died for us.
> Much more then, being now justified by his blood, we shall be saved from wrath through him.
> For if, when we were enemies, **we were reconciled** to God by the death of his Son, much more, being reconciled, we shall be saved by his life.

Since our "goodness" looks like filthiness to a holy God, we were totally without strength to save ourselves. The identity stamped on us was: sinner, enemy of God. *But God—* God had a plan to reconcile us to Himself. According to the dictionary, to reconcile means to restore friendly relations. How could an absolutely Holy God be on friendly terms with sinful humankind? In order to be reconciled to God, humankind needed a new identity, a new creation that only God could provide.

This provision is seen in the Person of God's Son. Just as God had to kill an innocent animal in Genesis three to cover Adam and Eve's shame, God would kill an innocent Lamb for the shame of all humankind. That Lamb that God killed in our place was His Son, Jesus Christ. God allowed Jesus to die as the perfect sacrifice in order to restore friendly relations with the humans who chose to reject Him.

Who would do such a thing? Who would you be willing to die for? As Romans five indicates, hardly anyone would do such a crazy thing as die for a good person, let alone for an enemy. Who in their right mind would be willing to die the death that his enemy deserves? Well, Jesus wasn't just willing to die the death that His enemies deserved. He did it! As Romans five puts it, God commended or proved his love for us when He died for us, his enemies. When we were without strength, while we were yet sinners, Christ died for me and for you. *You were that loved, that wanted, that worth it to God!*

Have you made the decision to trust Jesus as your personal Savior? If not, please realize that Jesus Christ has done all the work necessary to reconcile you with God. You can enter a relationship with God if you confess that you are a sinner, without strength to save yourself, and accept Jesus as your way to heaven and peace with God. When you admit that you are a sinner and trust in Jesus for forgiveness and salvation from sin, you receive Christ's perfection on your account. Guess what happens when you make this decision? Read these verses to find out:

▶ READ

John 1:12

> But as many as received him, to them gave he power to **become the sons of God**, even to them that believe on his name:

Romans 8:16-17

> The Spirit itself beareth witness with our spirit, that **we are the children of God.**
> And if children, then heirs; **heirs of God**, and **joint-heirs with Christ**; if so be that we suffer with him, that we may be also glorified together.

2 Corinthians 5:17, 21

> Therefore if any man be in Christ, **he is a new creature**: old things are passed away; behold, all things are become new.

> For he hath made him to be sin for us, who knew no sin; **that we might be made** the righteousness of God in him.

Galatians 4:4-7

> But when the fullness of the time was come, God sent forth his Son, made of a woman, made under the law.
> **To redeem them** that were under the law, that we might receive the **adoption of sons**.
> And because **ye are sons**, God hath sent forth the Spirit of his Son into your hearts, crying, Abba, Father.
> Wherefore thou art **no more a servant**, but a son; and if a son, then **an heir of God through Christ.**

Ephesians 2:13-16, 19

> **But now in Christ Jesus** ye who sometimes were far off are made nigh by the blood of Christ.
> For he is our peace, who hath made both one, and hath broken down the middle wall of partition between us;
> Having abolished in his flesh the enmity, even the law of commandments contained in ordinances; for to make in himself of twain **one new man**, so making peace;
> And **that he might reconcile both unto God in one body by the cross**, having slain the enmity thereby:

> Now therefore **ye are no more strangers** and foreigners, but fellowcitizens with the saints, and **of the household of God**;

Our New Identity

At salvation, you go through an identity change! No longer are you a marred creation serving the Devil. No longer does "damaged goods" define who you are. Because you have placed your faith in Jesus as your Savior, you are reclaimed by your Creator God and restored to a relationship with Him. Now when God looks down at you, He not only sees a precious creation of God, but He also sees a priceless child of God! What a wonderful, miraculous, and empowering new identity! Now, when someone asks you who you are, you can reply: "I'm God's child!" Along with this new identity comes a new ability through Christ. Let's check it out:

▶ **READ**

1 John 4:4

Ye are of God, little children, and have **overcome** them: because greater is he that is in you, than he that is in the world.

1 John 5:4-5

For whatsoever is born of God **overcometh** the world: and this is the victory that **overcometh** the world, **even our faith**.
Who is he that **overcometh** the world, but **he that believeth** that Jesus is the Son of God?

Philippians 2:13

For it is God which worketh in you both to will and to do of his good pleasure.

As Christians, we still fail at times. We still live in this sin-cursed world with the temptations and marks of Satan swirling around us every day. What is different about us after salvation? We have a new *belonging* and a new *power* to say no to Satan's wiles and wishes. Our new belonging is to God as an equal heir with Christ, and our new power is the Holy Spirit working in and through us.

When you place your faith in Christ as Savior, He places His Holy Spirit in you to guide and direct you to do right. We do not have to muster up strength from within ourselves and call upon our own willpower to resist Satan's temptations to sin. We can ask for the Holy Spirit's power to overcome sin. As Philippians 2:13 says, God is the one who gives us both the *want to and will do* in the battle to overcome sin. Yes, you are still in this dirty, scary, sin-cursed world, but *remember who you are!* Sin and your past no longer define you! You have Someone greater than Satan and sin living in you now. And Who does that Greater One say you are? God says you are an overcomer through your faith in Christ and the Holy Spirit.

We have all experienced the identity crisis of being a sin-marred creation of God. Yet we can all resolve that crisis by believing in Jesus Christ and Him alone to save and change us. If you haven't resolved this human problem of sin, won't you trust Jesus to save you and change you today? If you have already made that decision to trust Christ, won't you live in confidence of this new identity? All you have to do is claim that promise of power through the Holy Spirit and accept who you are in Christ: a child of God, an heir with Christ, and an overcomer of the world.

▶ Time to think!

HAVE YOU EVER MADE THE DECISION TO TRUST JESUS FOR FORGIVENESS AND SALVATION FROM SIN? IF SO, WHAT IS YOUR NEW IDENTITY, ACCORDING TO THE VERSES FROM THIS SECTION?

_____

_____

_____

AS A CHILD OF GOD, WHAT IS YOUR NEW BELONGING AND NEW POWER?

_____

_____

_____

WHAT IS ANOTHER WORD TO DESCRIBE YOUR NEW IDENTITY, FOUND IN I JOHN CHAPTERS FOUR AND FIVE?

_____

_____

_____

NOTES

"The I-surrender-all Christian life may be radical, but it is only reasonable."

4 "Remember Whose Kid You Are":
Our Purpose as God's Children

Have you ever had the pleasure of chatting with a "royal watcher"—one of those people obsessed with the latest news on the royal families? Somehow, we Americans find the concept of royalty romantic and fascinating. Although I don't keep up with the British royals, I do enjoy hearing about Prince William and Kate Middleton's growing little family. The most recent little royal welcomed into the world, Prince Louis Arthur Charles, is fifth in line for the British throne. While his future may look glamorous to all the "royal watchers" out there, little Prince Louis has the privilege and responsibility of living up to the royal family name and title. Because he would never wish to disgrace his family name or his nation's crown, he cannot live just to himself or for himself. He has the responsibility of representing his family name to the world.

Let's Start the Process

Do you realize that you are a royal too? When you asked Jesus Christ to be your Savior, you were welcomed into God's family. You went from being a servant of sin to being a son of God, an heir with Christ the King! While you may not be featured in the news headlines every week, your life is in the spotlight. Whether you feel the heat or not, your life is under scrutiny all the time because the world is watching. Your title as a child of God automatically makes you responsible to live up to that family name. Just as Prince Louis is distinct from the rest of the British population, so God's children are to be distinct and set apart from the world. Did God save us and give us a place in His family so we could live the same as we did before? The Bible is clear about the purpose for which we were saved:

▶ READ

Romans 6:1-7

> What shall we say then? Shall we continue in sin, that grace may abound?
> God forbid. How shall we, that are dead to sin, live any longer therein?
> Know ye not, that so many of us as were baptized into Jesus Christ were baptized into his death?
> Therefore we are buried with him by baptism into death: that like as Christ was raised up from the dead by the glory of the Father, **even so we also should walk in newness of life.**
> For if we have been planted together in the likeness of his death, we shall be also in the likeness of his resurrection:

Knowing this, that **our old man is crucified with him**, that the body of sin might be destroyed, that henceforth we should not serve sin.
For he that is dead is freed from sin.

Romans 8:29
For whom he did foreknow, **he also did predestinate to be conformed to the image of his Son**, that he might be the firstborn among many brethren.

God predetermined that those who accept Christ as Savior should begin a process of conforming to the image of Christ. *This process of becoming more like our King Jesus Christ is often called sanctification.* Sanctification is the purpose for which God saved us! As these verses indicate, sanctification is an ongoing process. So, how do we get this process started? Just as it did for Prince Louis in the royal family, the process of sanctification begins the moment you are born into God's family! This process progresses as we surrender to God's will for our lives, step by step, day after day. Now, as Christians, we hear about surrender to God's will often, but what does it mean practically?

The Step of Surrender

The thief is frantic, charging down the streets, throwing looks over his shoulder to see if they are still behind him. Yes, the police officers are right behind him, shouting the order to surrender. He takes a sharp right turn and then another, but his pursuers are not shaken off his trail. His lungs burning and his legs screaming for relief, the thief makes one last effort at escape. But he has taken the wrong turn. This time, his choice to go left instead of right has led him to a dead-end street. With nowhere else to turn and the police right behind him, the thief turns to face the police and throws up his hands in surrender.

Like a thief throwing his hands up, surrender means giving in to someone else's will. Surrender is submission to someone else's authority. None of us like the idea of surrender. Whether we are arguing a point, running from the police, or fighting in a war, we view surrender as a weakness and last resort. Every fiber of our being tells us never to surrender, never to give in, and never to put our hands up or out. We want to be self-ruled, self-dependent, self-existing. Yet none of us have ever been truly autonomous for one day in our lives! Whether we realize it or not, we are always listening, following, and obeying someone or something.

According to the Bible, the question is not *will we surrender*, but rather to whom *will we surrender*. We have the power of choice but not the power of autonomy. If we choose to live for ourselves and according to our own rules, we are really just living like puppet rulers, doing exactly what the Devil wanted us to do anyway. If we are not vulnerable and surrendered to God, we are left vulnerable and surrendered to sin and the Devil!

Before salvation, we were mindlessly following the Devil's way, without even realizing that our hands were held up in defeat to sin and out to our sinful whims. However, when we made the decision to trust Jesus as our Savior, we were freed from that bondage of sin. *We were freed to surrender to a different master.* God freed us so that we could hold our hands out to Him and allow Him to guide our lives! Next to trusting Jesus for salvation, surrendering our lives to God's will is the best decision we make.

▶ READ

Romans 6:16

> Know ye not, that to whom ye yield yourselves servants to obey, **his servants ye are** to whom ye obey; whether of sin unto death, or of obedience unto righteousness?

Romans 12:1-2

> I beseech you therefore, brethren, by the mercies of God, that ye present your bodies a living sacrifice, holy, acceptable unto God, **which is your reasonable service**.
> And be not **conformed** to this world: but be ye transformed by the renewing of your mind, that ye may prove what is that good, and acceptable, and perfect, **will of God**.

II Corinthians 5:14-15

> **For the love of Christ constraineth us;** because we thus judge, that if one died for all, then were all dead:
> And that he died for all, **that they which live should not henceforth live unto themselves, but unto him which died for them**, and rose again.

Colossians 3:1-4

> If ye then be risen with Christ, seek those things which are above, where Christ sitteth on the right hand of God.
> Set your affection on things above, not on things on the earth.
> For ye are dead, and **your life is hid with Christ** in God.
> When **Christ, who is our life**, shall appear, then shall ye also appear with Him in glory.

Now that we have seen that serving is not a choice, we must choose who we will serve. Many times, you and I are like the thief running from the police. We take something that doesn't belong to us—our lives—and we run away with it. While we think we have the right to do as we please with our lives, disregarding God's guidance in our lives is the same as stealing from God. Because God created our lives and redeemed our lives through Christ's death, He also has the right to guide our lives.

Sooner or later, like the thief, we will grow weary of running away with our own plans and designs for our lives. We will run into a dead end and then what? Why wait until our lungs are burning and our legs are dragging before we surrender to the One who has the right to our life anyway?

A Reasonable Choice

As Romans describes it, surrender to God's will for our lives is a reasonable choice. It only makes sense that the One who gives us breath today and heaven someday should be able to tell us what to do with our lives. Should the love of Christ—a love to the death—be enough to constrain us to surrender to God? As Colossians three puts it, Christ is literally our life. How foolish would it be to steal the life that God has so graciously granted us and wear ourselves out running from our loving God?

Like the thief, our only sensible choice is unconditional surrender. However, the parallel between us and the thief ends here. While the thief has prison to look forward to, you and I have liberty and fulfillment to look forward to. Starting the process of sanctification through surrender is the most freeing thing we can do. This sanctification—setting ourselves apart to God, surrendering our lives to Him—empowers us to live all out for Jesus Christ. Now, we not only have a basic human purpose as creations of God, but we have an eternal purpose as children of God! Everything we do in this life—our dreams and goals in life—should align with our purpose as God's child. Our career choices, family choices, and social choices should simply be tools used for the purpose of serving Christ, loving people, and sharing His gospel with others.

Our Reasonable Service

When we think of surrendering our lives to Christ and serving Him, full-time Christian ministry is what we usually think of. However, every Christian is a full-time Christian, no matter how he gets his paycheck. Whether we are full-time Christian school teachers or university professors, pastors or pastor's wives, full-time missionaries or mechanics, theologians or nurses at the local hospital, each of us should be involved in the local church, sharing Christ with our coworkers and raising our children to know Him. In fact, **the secular world needs more of our Christian influence.** Whatever we do, our identity is in Christ, and all we do should flow from our purpose to share Him with the world around us.

When we start the process of sanctification by taking that step of surrender, we are living out the purpose for which we were saved! Since you were worth dying for, God is worth living for. Since God gave His life for us, we have no right to live for ourselves. Jesus gave His life, so let's make Him our life. The I-surrender-all Christian life may be radical, but it is only reasonable.

▶ Time to think!

WHAT IS OUR PURPOSE FOR WHICH WE WERE SAVED?

_____

_____

_____

WHAT DOES SANCTIFICATION MEAN? WHEN DOES SANCTIFICATION START, AND WHAT PROGRESSES IT?

_____

_____

_____

IF WE ARE NOT SURRENDERED AND VULNERABLE TO GOD, TO WHAT AND TO WHOM ARE WE LEFT VULNERABLE?

_____

_____

_____

WHY SHOULD WE SURRENDER OUR LIVES TO CHRIST?

_____

_____

_____

IF YOU HAVE NEVER MADE THE DECISION TO SURRENDER YOUR LIFE TO GOD, WOULD YOU LIKE TO WRITE OUT A PRAYER OF SURRENDER AND SERVICE TO THE ONE WHO DIED FOR YOU?

_____

_____

_____

The Secret Weapon

It was the summer of 1940, and Britain felt alone in her stand against Hitler's conquest. The hum of Hitler's Luftwaffe in the London sky held the people below hostage in fear. The scream of sirens and the explosion of bombs terrorized Londoners every day during the Battle of Britain. That's when the British government finally decided to share with the United States a special secret.

The secret lay with a tiny device, about the size of a man's palm. This tiny device, the latest in radar technology, was called the *cavity magnetron*. The United States and Britain agreed to team up and use the cavity magnetron to create radar sets that could discreetly fit within Allied weapons, aircraft, and battle ships. This technology enabled Allied forces to detect the enemy aircraft, ships, or submarines that lurked miles away, even in the darkness. Historians have called this invention the Allies' "secret weapon" in the war against Hitler's conquest.

Once we have surrendered to God and are progressing in our sanctification, we have entered a war. We have just made war with a much bigger bully than Hitler was. And this enemy will fight fiercely during the process of sanctification. However, like Britain, we are not alone to face Satan's conquest. As Christians, we have a Secret Weapon in this war against sin and Satan. The name of our Secret Weapon is the Holy Spirit. The Holy Spirit is the one Who perceives the danger and tells us what our next move should be. He is the One with the power to enable us to make the right move and to do the right thing. Let's look at some ways that the Holy Spirit enables us in this fight against the Devil.

▶ READ

He gives assurance and confidence of salvation.
John 10:28-29

> And I give unto them eternal life; and they shall never perish, neither shall any man pluck them out of my hand.
>
> My Father, which gave them me, is greater than all; and no man is able to pluck them out of my Father's hand.

Romans 8:16
>The Spirit itself beareth witness with our spirit, that we are the children of God

Ephisians 1:13
>In whom ye also trusted, after that ye heard the word of truth, the gospel of your salvation: in whom also after that ye believed, **ye were sealed with that holy Spirit of promise,**

Ephesians 4:30
>And grieve not the **holy Spirit of God**, whereby **ye are sealed** unto the day of redemption.

1 John 5:13-14
>These things have I written unto you that believe on the name of the Son of God; that ye may know that ye have eternal life, and that ye may believe on the name of the Son of God.
>And this is **the confidence that we have in him**, that, if we ask anything according to his will, he heareth us:

He gives comfort and guidance in our lives.

John 14:16-18, 26
>And I will pray the Father, and he shall give you another Comforter, that he may abide with you forever;
>Even the Spirit of truth; whom the world cannot receive, because it seeth him not, neither knoweth him: but ye know him; for he dwelleth with you, and shall be in you.
>I will not leave you comfortless: I will come to you.
>
>But the Comforter, which is the Holy Ghost, whom the Father will send in my name, he shall teach you all things, and bring all things to your remembrance, whatsoever I have said unto you.

He fills us with strength to do right.

Romans 8:13, 26-27
>For if ye live after the flesh, ye shall die: but if ye through the Spirit do mortify the deeds of the body, ye shall live.
>
>Likewise the Spirit also helpeth our infirmities: for we know not what we should pray for as we ought: but the Spirit itself maketh intercession for us with groanings that cannot be uttered.

And he that searcheth the hearts knoweth what is the mind of the Spirit, because he maketh intercession for the saints according to the will of God.

Galatians 5:16
This I say then, **Walk in the Spirit**, and ye shall not fulfill the lust of the flesh.

Ephesians 3:16
That he would grant you, according to the riches of his glory, **to be strengthened with might by his Spirit in the inner man;**

Ephesians 5:18
And be not drunk with wine, wherein is excess; but **be filled with the Spirit**;

Ephesians 6:18
Praying always with all prayer and supplication **in the Spirit**, and watching thereunto with all perseverance and supplication for all saints;

Assurance

These passages paint the picture of our Secret Weapon in the fight against the Devil. One way that the Holy Spirit helps us is by giving us assurance of salvation. At the moment of salvation, the Holy Spirit seals us so that no one and nothing can take our salvation away. However, we can struggle with assurance of salvation. *Assurance means knowing for certain that our soul is safe with Jesus forever!* In contrast, a lack of assurance means that we lack confidence about whether we are saved or not. Our assurance may be shaky if we are living sinfully or focusing on our performance. Our feelings or other people's opinions can cause us to doubt our salvation, but we have a Secret Weapon to fight the doubt! When we look back to the Bible to see what God says about salvation, the Holy Spirit is there to testify to the truth that we are His and that we can never lose our salvation. The Bible explains in 1 John 5:9, *"If we receive the witness of men [our feelings, human opinions], the witness of God is greater [the Bible & Holy Spirit]: for this is the witness of God which he hath testified of his Son."* The basis for assurance is God's Word, not feelings, failures, or experiences. What got us saved in the first place (Jesus' work) is what keeps us saved (Jesus' work); and dwelling on this truth (Jesus' work) will also give us assurance of our own salvation. The ministry of the Holy Spirit gives us confidence that we are God's child and that nothing can ever change that.

Comfort and Guidance

Another way the Holy Spirit enables us is by comforting and teaching us. As we read the Bible, the Holy Spirit is there to teach us the truth, help us apply it to our lives, and live it out practically. When the disciples were troubled in John 14 at the news that Christ would soon leave earth, Jesus explained that the Holy Spirit would be their comfort, guide, and teacher—just as He had been while He was physically on earth. The process of sanctification requires the Holy Spirit's comfort, guidance, and teaching. The will of God and the conviction of Christ is manifested in the ministry of the Holy Spirit.

Filling

A third way that the Holy Spirit helps us in the fight is through filling us with strength to do right. As the Apostle Paul acknowledged in Romans 7, we do not in and of ourselves have the power to resist sin and do right. In Romans 7:18-19, Paul laments: "*For* **I know that in me** *(that is, in my flesh,)* **dwelleth no good thing**: *for to will is present with me; but how to perform that which is good I find not. For the good that I would I do not: but the evil which I would not, that I do.*" Paul then closes the chapter with this declaration: "*O wretched man that I am! who shall deliver me from the body of this death?*" (v. 24). The resolution to this predicament is found in the opening verses of Romans chapter 8: "*There is therefore now no condemnation to them which are in Christ Jesus, who walk not after the flesh, but* **after the Spirit**. *For* **the law of the Spirit** *of life in Christ Jesus* **hath made me free** *from the law of sin and death.* **For what the law could not do, in that it was weak through the flesh**, *God sending his own Son in the likeness of sinful flesh, and for sin, condemned sin in the flesh*: **That the righteousness of the law might be fulfilled in us**, *who walk not after the flesh,* **but after the Spirit**" (v. 1-4).

When we try to do right on our own, we are living as if we are still under the law and not under grace. When we focus on our performance as a Christian, we will fail and we may even doubt our salvation. But we were not saved so that we could continue living in the weakness of our own flesh. We were saved "that the righteousness of the law might be fulfilled in us" through the power of the Holy Spirit. Like Paul, we must admit our inability and yield to the Holy Spirit's filling to do right. While the Holy Spirit indwells us as a constant companion from the moment we trust Christ as Savior, He does not always fill us. The filling of the Holy Spirit happens when we invite Him to sit on the throne of our hearts to control and guide our attitudes and actions. When we ask our constant companion, the Holy Spirit, to fill us, He provides everything we need to progress in our sanctification and stave off Satan.

◗ Time to think!

WHAT IS OUR SECRET WEAPON DURING THE PROCESS OF SANCTIFICATION THAT HELPS US FIGHT AGAINST THE DEVIL?

_____

_____

_____

WHAT ARE THREE WAYS THAT THE HOLY SPIRIT HELPS US IN THE FIGHT AGAINST SIN AND THE DEVIL?

_____

_____

_____

WHAT IS ASSURANCE? WHAT IS THE BASIS FOR ASSURANCE AND WHO GIVES US THAT ASSURANCE?

_____

_____

_____

WHAT IS THE INDWELLING OF THE HOLY SPIRIT AND WHAT IS THE FILLING OF THE HOLY SPIRIT?

_____

_____

_____

Remember Whose You Are

Who you belong to informs how you act. Your identity informs your purpose. For example, I remember as a young child, when my parents would leave me with a babysitter, my dad would crouch down, look me in the eye, and say with a smile, "Remember whose kid you are!" I would always laugh and nod. Of course, Dad wasn't afraid that I'd have amnesia and forget who my parents were! But Dad knew that if I remembered who I belonged to, it would help me remember how to act. Dad expected me to live up to the family name.

Just like my dad, our heavenly Father wants us to remember whose kids we are. So far in this study, we have learned that our identity in Christ is child of God and heir with the King. And that identity informs us that our purpose is to progress in our sanctification—through surrender and the Holy Spirit. Just as a prince is quick to tell people that his father is the king, we should be excited to tell people about our new identity in Christ!

"There may not be a flood coming, but there is a King coming and we are on His side!"

5 "Stay Salty?": Our Purpose as Noahs

> **READ**
> Genesis 6

Do you remember having a first impression of Noah's story? If your first time hearing about Noah and the Ark was in children's church, the blow was probably somewhat softened. But when you read Genesis six without the storybook pictures of a little ark and cute animals poking their heads out of the windows, you realize just how catastrophic the story is. When I first read Genesis chapter six without the flash card pictures, my initial reaction was—*Harsh!!! How could God just destroy everything and everyone He'd just created only a few chapters before?* However, God is not the One taking drastic measures in Genesis six. As we have read, God gave mankind 120 years advance warning of His impending judgement. While God was reasonably acting within His character of holiness, people were colorfully displaying their sinful cores.

In Genesis chapters three and four are recorded the first murders and the practice of polygamy! Genesis chapter five records Adam's descendants, and then we find ourselves in chapter six—Noah's world. Within a few generations, people had strayed so far from their original purpose as God's creations—they had grown so sinful—that God sighed heavily at the thought of them! What had happened in just a few generations to make God so opposed to His crowning creation? Tragically, the problem of Noah's day is the same problem of our day.

Although God has promised never to destroy the world with a flood again, our world cannot go on forever. Jesus Christ will return as King one day and rain judgement on the world we now know. However, the answer to this deep-seated problem that our world and Noah's world both share is the same. We Christians don't need to feel pessimistic or fearful about our wicked world and wait idly for Christ's return. Instead, we need to roll up our sleeves and get busy!

Identify the Problem

Before we can guard against it in our own lives, we must first identity the problem of Noah's world. While God does not record in great detail the sins of Noah's day, He does mention where all the chaotic wickedness started. This simple sin should send up red flags in our brains.

▶ READ

Genesis 6:1-2, 5, 12

And it came to pass, when men began to multiply on the face of the earth, and daughters were born unto them,
That the sons of God saw the daughters of men that they were fair; and they took them wives of all which they chose.

And GOD saw that the wickedness of man was great in the earth, and that every imagination of the thoughts of his heart was **only evil continually.**

And God looked upon the earth, and, behold, it was corrupt; **for all flesh had corrupted his way upon the earth.**

From these verses we can identify the problem of Noah's world. Yes, the verses say that the people of the world were "only evil continually" and that their way was "corrupt." But what landed them in that predicament? Verses one and two clue us in: it was the simple sin of distraction from God's way that landed Noah's world in its state of absolute perversion! God's *way is His design for life—* how He intends His creation to operate. *Perversion is taking God's creation and twisting it into something that God did not intend.* Distraction from God's way and perversion of God's creation go hand in hand.

This vicious cycle of distraction and perversion was first illustrated in Genesis chapter three when Adam and Eve introduced sin into the world. How did the fall of man happen? Adam and Eve did not wake up to their perfect world one day and decide in their hearts to rebel against the God with Whom they had been fellowshipping. No, Eve simply walked through the garden one day, looked the wrong way, and became distracted with an attractive fruit and talking serpent!

Eve's distraction from God's way led to perversion of God's way. She took the fruit that God had created and used it for a purpose that He had not intended. The fruit was not intrinsically wrong—God had created it Himself! What made it wrong was Eve taking the fruit outside of God's design and using it to fulfill her own desires. Simple distraction led to inviting sin into the world.

The same scenario is played for us in the opening of Genesis chapter six. When the sons of God (believers) became distracted with the daughters of men (unbelievers), they followed their lustful passions and married unbelievers (daughters of men). That was the first step away from God's way and toward perversion. Passing time blurred the distinction between God's people and unbelievers. Before long, believers and unbelievers alike were participating in all kinds of violence and perversion. Eventually, the believing generation died out, leaving only a remnant of righteous—Noah and his family.

This same cycle of distraction and perversion is happening in our modern culture. Both believers and unbelievers in our world today have completely abandoned God's way for life. From marriage and family to entertainment and social activities, people have *allowed their lustful passions to turn God's gifts into perversions.* Homosexuality has been embraced and flaunted to the world. Premarital sex has been normalized. Murder is old news. Drug wars ravage everywhere.

Most tragically, modern Christians are not immune to this cycle of distraction and perversion. Christians have allowed their own lustful passions to drag them from God's way and have submissively accepted the sins of the world around them.

▶ READ

Genesis 6:8-13

> **But Noah found grace** in the eyes of the LORD.
> These are the generations of Noah: Noah was a just man and perfect in his generations, and Noah walked with God.
> And Noah begat three sons, Shem, Ham, and Japeth.
> The earth also was corrupt before God, and the earth was filled with violence.
> And God looked upon the earth, and, behold, it was corrupt; for all flesh had corrupted his way upon the earth.
> And God said unto Noah, The end of all flesh is come before me; for the earth is filled with violence through them; and, behold, I will destroy them with the earth.

Amidst the corruption and violence of his world, Noah stood out to God. Unlike the masses around him, Noah faithfully walked with God and raised a family to do the same. Can you help but wonder how many faithful believers God would find in our world today? Well, in Genesis chapter six, God found only one faithful man.

How was it possible for one man and his family to remain righteous in God's eyes when the rest of world was literally decaying in sin? With all the corruption swirling around them, the righteousness of Noah's family did not just happen by accident. Noah had to be proactive about protecting himself and his family from corruption. He had to choose to eliminate distractions of his world and focus on God's way. Because of Noah's choice to eliminate distractions and because of His faithfulness to God's way, God spared Noah and his family from judgement. As a result, the entire human race was preserved!

If we want to be the Noahs of our day, we must make the same choice to eliminate distractions. Every day is a new battle as we are bombarded with corrupt music, images, advertisements, and propositions that threaten to distract us from God's way. If we give in to these distractions and indulge in the world's corruption, we will only add to the confusion and wickedness that is destroying our world. Unchecked appetites for sin must be quenched. We must erect borders in our lives to keep us from coddling attractions to worldly entertainment and experimenting with worldly lifestyles. Even the people we choose to hang out with must never become a distraction from God's way.

Why does it matter so much? Because there is a battle to win. There may not be a flood coming; but *there is a King coming, and we are on His side!* We are called to take on the challenge of being the Noahs of our day. No more playing around with distractions—it's time to commit to staying on track with God's way.

▶ Time to think!

HOW IS GOD'S WAY DEFINED? HOW IS PERVERSION DEFINED?

_____
_____
_____

WHAT WAS THE PROBLEM (SIN) OF NOAH'S DAY?

_____
_____
_____

WHAT ARE SOME DISTRACTIONS THREATENING TO TAKE YOU AWAY FROM GOD'S WAY THAT YOU NEED TO ELIMINATE FROM YOUR LIFE?

_____
_____
_____

Emulating Noah's Position

In addition to identifying the problem of Noah's day, we must emulate the position that Noah took in his world. Our modern world is not far behind the level of wickedness that Noah's world had reached. As Matthew 24:37 says, *"But as the days of Noe were, so shall also the coming of the Son of man be."* As the return of Christ nears, the world will continue toward corruption. However, the continued perversion of our world does not give us a free pass to be disengaged and mind our own business until Christ returns! As the Noahs of our day, we have a vital responsibility to our world. The position that Noah took and the position we should emulate is articulated in these verses:

▶ Read

Hebrews 11:7

> By faith Noah, being warned of God of things not seen as yet, moved with fear, prepared an ark to the saving of his house; by the which he condemned the world, and became heir of the righteousness which is by faith.

Matthew 5:13-16

> **Ye are the salt of the earth**: but if the salt have lost its savour, wherewith shall it be salted? it is thenceforth good for nothing, but to be cast out, and to be trodden under foot of men.
> **Ye are the light of the world**. A city that is set on an hill cannot be hid. Neither do men light a candle, and put it under a bushel, but on a candlestick; and it giveth light unto all that are in the house.
> Let your light so shine before men, that they may see your good works, and glorify your Father which is in heaven.

How Salty Are You?

Our purpose as Noahs of our day is to be the salt that preserves and the light that shines God's truth to the world around us. To be salt means to give the world a taste of righteousness. Just like salt preserves and enhances the flavor of whatever food it is put on, salty Christians preserve the flavor of righteousness and enhance God's way in the world around them.

Our perverted world is starved for righteousness! Too many people with whom we rub shoulders every day have no idea what God's way looks like. They've never had a taste of righteousness!

If we lose our saltiness, we will fail to fulfill our purpose as God's children. As Jesus emphasized in Matthew five, there is nothing more worthless than saltless salt! Our world doesn't need more saltless Christians; no, our world desperately needs salty Christians like Noah. As Noahs of our day, we are commanded to give our world the flavor of righteousness.

How Bright Are You?

As lights of the world, we are called to be the stark contrast, the shining difference from the darkness of this sinful world. Everything we do in our lives should shed light on the truth of God's Word and the Person of Jesus Christ. Many people in our dark world stumble through life thinking that sin is the only way to live. They have never glimpsed the light of God's way! Yet if they come into contact with Christians, they should see a stark contrast—they should see Jesus and His way.

How ridiculous would it be to light a candle, only to hide its light under a bushel! That's how ridiculous it is for Christians to dim their lights out of fear of being different. The entire purpose of our Christian light is to brightly light the way to Jesus Christ! In so doing, we will be fulfilling our most basic purpose of glorifying God.

Be a Noah

Like Noah, we have the opportunity to hold off God's judgement just a little longer. It may be 120 years, or it may be 20 years, 20 days, or 20 hours before Christ returns as King. Whatever our allotted time, we must be as salty and as bright as we can be in order to win more people to God's way. Let's not swallow the lie that our world is too far gone and that our saltiness and brightness do not make a difference for eternity. If anyone had an excuse to be discouraged, it would have been Noah.

In our modern world, we certainly don't face anything worse than Noah did, and we will most certainly see more fruit for our labors. We cannot afford to lose our saltiness when we are the only taste of righteousness our world will get. How dare we dim our lights when we are the ones to show others that there is a better way to live—God's way! Let's not fear, and let's not give up on our world! Instead, let's fulfill our purpose as the Noahs of our day, staying salty and shining brightly in our desperate and darkening world.

▶ Time to think!

WHAT IS OUR PURPOSE AS NOAHS OF OUR DAY (I.E. AS SALT AND LIGHT)?

_____

_____

_____

WHAT ARE SOME FEARS OR ATTITUDES SEEKING TO LESSEN YOUR SALTINESS OR DIM YOUR LIGHT?

_____

_____

_____

"Your story is a crucial part of the body of Christ."

6 Colors of the Rainbow:
Finding Purpose in Second Chances

On the morning of October 2, 2017, I woke up to the news of the deadliest mass shooting in America's history. Along with thousands of other Americans, my heart was broken. Just an hour before the shooting began, the crowd had joined country stars Big & Rich in singing "God Bless America." A Las Vegas country concert that had begun three days earlier as an event for Americans to enjoy together, had ended as a national tragedy!

No words could describe the sadness over so much loss of life at once—over 50 dead and over 400 injured. The numbers were almost as staggering as the fact that someone could commit such a heinous crime! Yet the human capacity for heroism displayed that night was amazing, too. A man named Sonny Melton, a nurse from Tennessee, shielded his wife from the gunfire with his own body. He lost his life in the process of saving hers. One lady called a metro officer her guardian angel because he stayed with her and shielded her until she was able to get out of the venue. Another victim recounted the heroism of his sister who threw herself on top of him when the shots rang out, repeating, "I love you, Taylor, I love you." In Taylor's words: "I went into that concert an agnostic, and left a firm believer in God." Like many others on that horrible night, Taylor was given a second chance at life—a chance that Taylor knew came from the hand of God.

The God of Second Chances

As He did for Taylor in 2017, God gave a second chance to the entire human race in Genesis chapter eight. As we have read in the previous chapters, after hundreds of years of free will coupled with Adam's sinful core, humankind had completely rejected God's original purpose for them. Genesis six describes the people's thoughts as "only evil continually." The only salty, God-fearing, bright-shining person God could find in that day was Noah.

God had stayed His judgment for the sake of righteousness, but justice could not be stayed forever. As Holy God, the Lord destroyed the earth and every living thing, saving Noah and his family in the ark. In just one chapter, in just 150 days, the entire landscape of the world changed. Life would never be the same again, but there would be life again. Because while God is the Righteous Judge of the Universe, He is also the God of second chances.

▶ Read

Genesis 8:1, 21

> **And God remembered Noah,** and every living thing, and all the cattle that was with him in the ark: and God made a wind to pass over the earth, and the waters assuaged;
>
> And the LORD smelled a sweet savor; and the LORD said in his heart, I will not again curse the ground any more for man's sake; for the imagination of man's heart is evil from his youth; neither will I again smite any more every thing living, as I have done.

Genesis 9:1, 12-17

> **And God blessed Noah** and his sons, and said unto them, Be fruitful, and multiply, and replenish the earth.
>
> And God said, This is the token of the covenant which I make between me and you and every living creature that is with you, for perpetual generations: I do set my bow in the cloud, and it shall be for a token of a covenant between me and the earth.
> And it shall come to pass, when I bring a cloud over the earth, that the bow shall be seen in the cloud:
> And I will remember my covenant, which is between me and you and every living creature of all flesh; and the waters shall no more become a flood to destroy all flesh.
> And the bow shall be in the cloud; and I will look upon it, that I may remember the everlasting covenant between God and every living creature of all flesh that is upon the earth.
> And God said unto Noah, This is the token of the covenant, which I have established between me and all flesh that is upon the earth.

Noah's Second Chance

Chapter eight opens with the phrase, "*And God remembered Noah.*" If you're like me, you may be scratching your head, saying, What? If God can't forget anything, how can He remember? When the Bible says that God remembered Noah, it simply means that God still had a purpose and a plan for Noah. God called Noah and his family out of the ark and gave them the command to replenish the earth. Even after humankind had failed Him so badly, God wanted to fill up His world with humans again! He wanted to love them, know them, and fellowship with them. To seal His covenant with humankind, God placed a colorful rainbow in the sky. Throughout the ages, this colorful reminder has graced the sky, representing God's faithfulness in giving second chances.

Just take a moment to consider all the second chances God has handed out to people we know in the Bible. Abraham had a son with a servant girl, but God still came through and delivered the promised son, Isaac. In a fit of rage, Moses murdered an Egyptian and then ran away to hide for years in the desert. Still, God commissioned Moses to lead the people of Israel out of slavery. Even though Rahab had lived her life as a harlot, God responded to her repentance. Not only did God spare Rahab's life, but He even gave her a place in the lineage of Jesus Christ! Ruth grew up as an idol-worshipper, yet God also gave her the privilege of being in the lineage of King David and Jesus Christ! Jonah, the runaway prophet, experienced God's mercy and finished the task he was sent for. Even King David experienced second, third, and fourth chances after he messed up royally and asked for God's forgiveness! God is always faithful to keep His promises to us. We are the ones who tend to mess things up.

While the Bible characters mentioned above made good use of their second chances, others in the Bible wasted their second chances. For example, Sampson was given many chances to live out His God-given purpose as a Nazarite, but he continued to waste them with foolish living. In the end, Sampson died in the presence of his enemies. Ruth's sister-in-law, Orpah, was given the same chance to live with God's people that Ruth was given, but Orpah chose to stay with her pagan people. Lot's wife was given the chance to escape the burning Sodom and Gomorrah, yet she chose to look back. Many times, God reached out to King Saul, but Saul continued to disregard God's voice until a day came when he could no longer hear it. The list could go on, but this list should be enough to warn us that we could waste our second chances if we fail to learn from others' mistakes.

Purpose in Second Chances

As Christians, we have been given the ultimate second chance at life with God. Throughout our Christian life, we may stray off the path, but God is always waiting and ready to hand out a second chance to those who want one. As long as God gives you breath, you have purpose on this earth. So, how can we make good use of the second chances God gives us? We can learn what our purpose is in second chances if we consider how Noah responded to his second chance.

▶ Read

Genesis 8:20-22

> And Noah built an altar unto the LORD; and took of every clean beast, and of every clean fowl, and offered burnt offerings on the altar.
> And the LORD smelled a sweet savour; and the LORD said in his heart, I will not again curse the ground any more for man's sake; for the imagination of man's heart is evil from his youth; neither will I again smite any more

every thing living, as I have done.

While the earth remaineth, seedtime and harvest, and cold and heat, and summer and winter, and day and night shall not cease.

Seek and Thank God

The first thing that Noah did with his second chance was thank God for it. Unlike Sampson who disregarded God's second chances, Noah recognized his second chance as a gift from God. Noah expressed His recognition of and thankfulness to God with a burnt offering.

The first step to finding purpose in our second chances is to seek God and thank Him for His involvement in our lives. God wants to use the second chances in our lives to deepen our relationship with Him and to reveal His involvement in our lives. Remember Taylor's second chance story? As Taylor realized from his harrowing experience, God gives second chances in order to reach out to us and to encourage us to seek Him and know Him. Every interaction God has with His creation is for the purpose of revealing Himself to us. While we often have the misconception that God has left us or is hiding from us, God never wishes to hide Himself from us. We are the ones who hide from God. It has been this way since the day Adam and Eve hid themselves in fig leaves. God was not the One who hid when Adam and Eve sinned. When God entered the garden that evening, He sought for Adam and Eve, calling out, "*Where art thou?*" (Genesis 3:9). Although God knew where they were, He did not force Himself on them. God wanted Adam and Eve to choose to stop the futile attempts of hiding from Him and choose to seek Him as well! He gave them a second chance because He wanted to have a relationship with them. Since God is always there for us, the first step we can take to make good use of our second chances is to seek Him and thank Him for His involvement in our lives. As the verses below indicate, if you look for God, you will find Him! Every time.

▶ Read

Jeremiah 29:12-13

> Then shall ye call upon me, and ye shall go and pray unto me, and I will hearken unto you.
>
> **And ye shall seek me, and find me,** when ye shall search for me with all your heart.

Psalm 73:28

> But it is good for me to draw near to God: I have put my trust in the Lord GOD, that I may declare all thy works.

Hebrews 11:6-7

> But without faith it is impossible to please him: for he that cometh to God must believe that he is, and that **he is a rewarder of them that diligently seek him**.
> By faith Noah, being warned of God of things not seen as yet, moved with fear, prepared an ark to the saving of his house; by the which he condemned the world, and became heir of the righteousness which is by faith.

From these verses, we see that God gives second chances so that we will call upon Him (Jeremiah 29:12-13) and so that we will draw closer to Him (Psalm 73:28). Drawing near to God takes faith on our part, but as Hebrews 11:6 promises, God rewards those brave souls who seek Him. Like Noah, we must exercise the faith we do have, whether we consider it to be big or small. And like Noah, we must seek God and thank God for His involvement in our lives. If you are wondering why God seems like a distant acquaintance, remember that God never does the leaving. While we each have a unique story, like Taylor, our first step to making good use of our second chances is to seek Him and thank Him for His involvement in our lives. As the old hymn goes:

Then with my waking thoughts, bright with thy praise
Out of my stony griefs, Bethel I raise;
So by my woes to be Nearer, my God to Thee,
Or if on joyful wing, Cleaving the sky,
Sun, moon, and stars forgot, Upward I'll fly,
Still all my song shall be, Nearer, my God, to Thee,
Nearer, my God, to thee, Nearer to Thee!

▶ Time to think!

WHAT WAS THE FIRST THING NOAH DID WITH HIS SECOND CHANCE?

_____

_____

_____

WHAT IS OUR FIRST STEP TO MAKING GOOD USE OF OUR SECOND CHANCES?

___

___

___

WHAT ARE SOME MISCONCEPTIONS YOU MAY HAVE HAD ABOUT GOD DURING A TRIAL?

___

___

___

Continuing on the Right Track

We have seen that the first step to finding purpose in our second chances is to seek God and thank Him for His involvement in our lives, but now we must continue on the right track. How can we protect ourselves from falling away into the same sin that required God's grace in the first place? Well, one example of how not to use the gift of a second chance is the story of King Saul.

▶ Read

I Samuel 13:11-14

And Samuel said, What hast thou done? And Saul said, Because I saw that the people were scattered from me, and that thou camest not within the days appointed, and that the Philistines gathered themselves together at Michmash;
Therefore said I, The Philistines will come down now upon me to Gilgal, and I have not made supplication unto the LORD: I forced myself therefore, and offered a burnt offering.
And Samuel said to Saul, Thou hast done foolishly: thou hast not kept the commandment of the LORD thy God, which he commanded thee: for now would the LORD have established thy kingdom upon Israel for ever.
But now thy kingdom shall not continue: the LORD hath sought him a man

after his own heart, and the LORD hath commanded him to be captain over his people, because thou hast not kept that which the LORD commanded thee.

Ask for a Clean Heart

In this passage, we see that Saul feigned sorrow for his sin and asked forgiveness of the prophet Samuel. Yet he never changed because he never asked God to forgive and cleanse his heart. In contrast, while David made many mistakes, he was a man after God's own heart. Unlike Saul, David made good use of his second chances because he asked God to cleanse his heart. We can't afford to live our lives like Saul. Living in our own strength and changing by our own power never works. We need to be people after God's own heart, like David. How can we be after God's own heart if we don't ask God to change our heart?

The second step to finding purpose in our second chances is to pray for a clean heart. Only when we have a genuine clean heart can we have a genuine life change! We cannot expect to bounce back into a right relationship with God if we do not ask for His power to change our heart. Our hearts will lead us right back down the wrong path that required God's trial in our lives in the first place. Neither can we determine to change by our own strength. Plenty of people in the Bible prove that human strength does not change the human heart. Only God can change hearts and He will if we ask Him to on a regular basis. As Saul found out, God does not want our sacrifices, our appeasement, or our vain promises to do better. God wants our hearts!

▶ Read

Jeremiah 17:9-10
> The heart is deceitful above all things, and desperately wicked: who can know it?
> I the LORD search the heart, I try the reins, even to give every man according to his ways, and according to the fruit of his doings.

Psalm 44:21
> Shall not God search this out? **for he knoweth the secrets of the heart**.

Psalm 51:10, 16-17
> **Create in me a clean heart,** O God; and renew a right Spirit within me.

> For thou desirest not sacrifice; else would I give it: thou delightest not in burnt offering.
> **The sacrifices of God are a broken spirit: a broken and a contrite heart,** O God, thou wilt not despise.

Passing It On

When we consider Noah's story, we see that God didn't spare Noah and his family so that they could live in a little commune and keep to themselves. No, God wanted them to multiply and replenish the earth. He wanted them to tell their children and grandchildren and great grandchildren the story about how mankind messed things up but how God offered a second chance. As Noah did, *another purpose we can find in second chances is passing on our story to others.*

▶ Read

Psalm 73:28
> But it is good for me to draw near to God: I have put my trust in the Lord GOD, that I may **declare** all thy works.

Hebrews 10:23-24
> Let us hold fast the **profession** of our faith without wavering; (for he is faithful that promised;)
> And let us consider one another to provoke unto love and to good works:

I Thessalonians 5:11
> Wherefore comfort yourselves together, and **edify one another**, even as also ye do.

Tell Your Story

As these verses indicate, God did not bring us safely through a trial and offer us a second chance just so we could go on our merry way and never tell another soul about what God has done for us. One of the best ways to waste a second chance is to keep it to yourself! Have you ever engaged in your church's testimony time or listened to a candidate's campaign speech or even watched an insurance commercial on television? Something each of these scenarios has in common is storytelling! People are not always convinced to believe in something (or Someone) because of hard, cold facts. But people are swayed by other people's personal experiences.

The purpose of your second chance—your story—is to encourage other people to believe God and trust Him with their lives. Your story is a crucial part of the body of Christ, and you should use it to help fellow Christians strengthen their own faith in God and to stir them up to good works! God's gift of a second chance shouldn't end with you, but it should be extended through you to others. There is a much bigger picture than just you and your life.

Perhaps you know a friend who is going through a trial, testing, or time of correction from God. Maybe you can sense that they are forming misconceptions about God and holding bitterness against God. Don't let them fend for themselves! Get to know them, reach out to them, and express to them how God used a trial, testing, or time of correction in your own life. Explain to them how God provided a second chance for you and what produced the change in your life! Point them back to God so that their faith can be strengthened and their second chance can be accepted and used for the glory of God. Next time you admire the colors of the rainbow, remember that God is the Giver of second chances. Seek Him, thank Him, and share Him with others.

▶ Time to think!

WHAT ARE TWO OTHER PURPOSES WE CAN FIND IN SECOND CHANCES?

_____

_____

_____

DO YOU NEED TO PRAY FOR A HEART CHANGE BEFORE YOU CAN SEE A LIFE CHANGE? IF SO, WHY DON'T YOU WRITE DOWN A PRAYER TO GOD RIGHT NOW:

_____

_____

_____

DO YOU KNOW SOMEONE WHO NEEDS TO HEAR ABOUT WHAT GOD DID IN YOUR LIFE? IF SO, WRITE DOWN THEIR NAME; PRAY FOR THEM AND FOR AN OPPORTUNITY TO SHARE YOUR STORY WITH THEM!

_____

_____

_____

NOTES

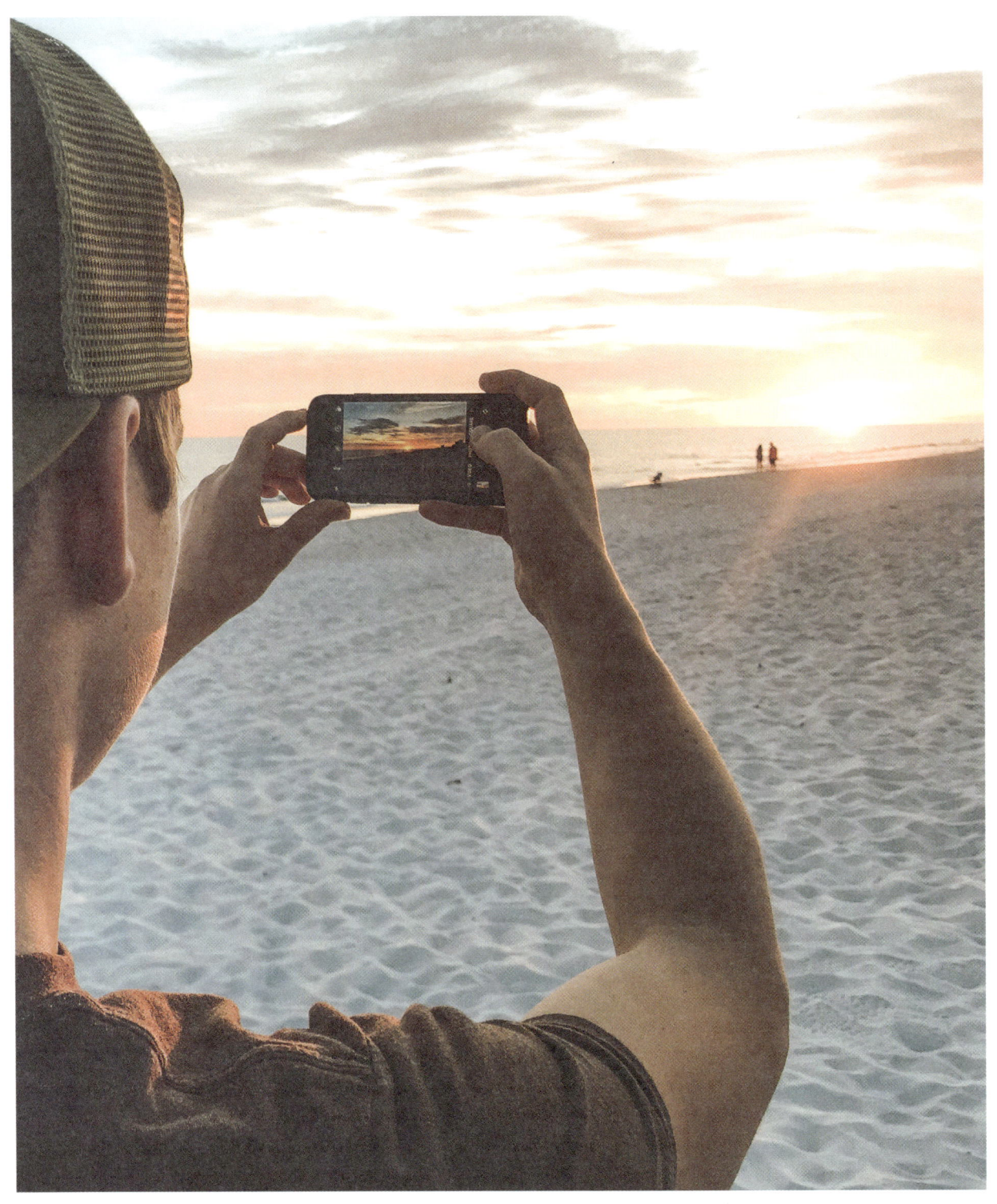

"Humility is a singular upward focus on God and an acceptance of His estimation of us."

7 "That Looks Good on You!": A Biblical Perspective of Self-Esteem

Chloe had thirty minutes before she had to be out the door for the senior banquet. Despite her best efforts to plan ahead, the day had flown away and she still didn't know what to wear on her big night! With a moan, she threw open her closet and fingered through several dresses. She pulled out a blue one, looked in the mirror from every angle, estimated her appearance, and scowled. Nope, not right. Next, she tried on a pink one and called in her sister for a second opinion. Still not the one. The exhausting cycle continued through five more dresses until, finally, Chloe donned the last one in her closet.

"Now that looks good on you!" exclaimed Chloe's sister.

Chloe's face brightened and everything seemed to be okay again. She was going to the banquet, and she was feeling good about it too!

Self-esteem—it's not something we talk about often, but it's something all of us have. Do you have a high self-esteem or a low self-esteem? Perhaps it is difficult to answer that question without first defining the term. Self-esteem is your evaluation of yourself, what you believe or think about yourself. It's like when you try on an outfit, look in the mirror, and make an estimation of how you look in it. Your estimation of yourself influences your decision, actions, and interactions with others.

In Genesis chapter eleven, we find a group of people who had very high self-esteem. In fact, they thought so highly of themselves that they believed they could climb as high as heaven! They thought they could lift themselves up to God's level.

▶ Read

Genesis 11:1-9

And the whole earth was of one language, and of one speech.

And it came to pass, as they journeyed from the east, that they found a plain in the land of Shinar; and they dwelt there.

And they said one to another, Go to, let us make brick, and burn them thoroughly. And they had brick for stone, and slime had they for mortar.

And they said, Go to, let us build us a city and a tower, whose top may reach unto heaven; and **let us make us a name**, lest we be scattered abroad upon the face of the whole earth.

And the LORD came down to see the city and the tower, which the children of men builded.

And the LORD said, Behold, the people is one, and they have all one language; and this they begin to do: and now nothing will be restrained from

> them, which they have imagined to do.
> Go to, let us go down, and there confound their language, that they may not understand one another's speech.
> So the LORD scattered them abroad from thence upon the face of all the earth: and they left off to build the city.
> Therefore is the name of it called Babel; because the LORD did there confound the language of all the earth: and from thence did the LORD scatter them abroad upon the face of all the earth.

After a globe-transforming flood, God wanted to see the earth bustling with people again. His command to Noah's family was to multiply and replenish the earth, the *entire* earth. However, in Genesis eleven, the entire population is clustered together in one place as one nation. Feeling strong in their unity and numbers, the people of the earth planned to construct a tower that touched heaven. The people clearly stated their goal in verse four: "*Let us make us a name, lest we be scattered abroad upon the face of the whole earth*" (v.4). Rather than live in obedience to God's command to spread out and fill the earth, these people wanted to stick together and make a name for themselves!

Because of their folly, God interrupted their building with chaos. He confounded their languages so that the frustrated builders would seek out other people who understood their language. The people of like languages left the tower project and spread out upon the face of the earth—just as God had intended in the first place.

Defining the Terms

The problem that infected the people of the earth in Genesis eleven is the same infectious disease that eats away at people today. Perhaps C.S. Lewis most accurately describes this problem in his book *Mere Christianity*: "For pride is spiritual cancer: it eats up the very possibility of love, or contentment, or even common sense." Oh, how that statement sums up the story that unfolds at the tower of Babel! As we read this story, it is easy for us to laugh at these people's folly. But can we identify folly when it flares up in our own lives?

We humans think that pride looks ugly on everyone else but ourselves. After all, we are really good at finding a rationale for our own pride. In our minds, humility either means we feel pitiful, or it means that we are weak.

This misconception of humility has caused many people to stumble and many kingdoms to fall. God calls us to be humble, but not because he wants us to be pitiful or weak. God doesn't want us to suffer from low self-esteem any more than He wants us to suffer from high self-esteem. Neither does God call us to be humble because it is the height of virtue. What, then, is the purpose of being humble? Why should we be humble? Let's consider what is the proper definition of humility and what is our purpose in humility.

Read

Psalm 34:2
> My soul shall make her boast in the LORD: the humble shall hear thereof, and be glad. [Humility delights in exalting God.]

Proverbs 18:12
> Before destruction the heart of man is haughty, and before honour is humility.

Proverbs 22:4
> By humility and the fear of the LORD are riches, and honour, and life. [Humility puts the fear of the Lord before all else.]

Zephaniah 2:3
> Seek ye the LORD, all ye meek of the earth, which have wrought his judgment; seek righteousness, seek meekness: it may be ye shall be hid in the day of the LORD'S anger. [Humility is a singular seeking of God.]

Pride: Looks Down

From these verses, we see that self-esteem—humility and pride—are simply matters of focus, direction, and perspective. For example, pride looks down on everyone and everything else. Remember why the people in Genesis chapter eleven built the tower? They built it, not to worship God, but to disobey God. Their actions were a form of self-worship and the epitome of pride. No sin would have been committed in building an amazing structure in honor of God—if it had been, in fact, built solely for His honor. The problem arose when the *why* behind the project was self-worship or an attempt at self-affirmation. Likewise, if we are working "for God" in order to make ourselves known on the one hand or working "for God" in order to make ourselves worth something on the other hand—both are futile and both are prideful. Pride is simply a self-focus.

Humility: Looks Up

In contrast, humility is a perspective and a focus that looks up. Again, C.S. Lewis explained it best when he said, "Humility is not thinking less of yourself; it's thinking of yourself less." Humility cannot mean looking down on yourself, hating yourself, or feeling sorry for yourself because all those emotions arise out of self-focus.

As seen in the previous verses in Psalms and Proverbs, humility means thinking about God more than we think about ourselves. Humility delights in exalting and praising

God. Humility prioritizes God's Word and God's will above all else in life and seeks God first and foremost. Humility is a singular looking up to God. When our focus is God alone, everything else in life is seen in the proper light. Let us consider some Bible examples of a proper view of God, self, and others.

▶ Read

I Kings 18:36

> And it came to pass at the time of the offering of the evening sacrifice, that Elijah the prophet came near, and said, LORD God of Abraham, Isaac, and of Israel, let it be known this day that thou art God in Israel, and that **I am thy servant**, and that **I have done all these things at thy word**. [Elijah gives God the credit for all his miracles and identifies God as his Master.]

Isaiah 64:8

> But now, O LORD, **thou art our father; we are the clay**, and thou our potter; and we all are the work of thy hand. [Isaiah identifies God as our Father and Creator.]

Luke 1:46-55

> And Mary said, My soul doth magnify the Lord,
> And my spirit hath rejoiced in God my Savior.
> For **he hath regarded the low estate of his handmaiden: for, behold, from henceforth all generations shall call me blessed.**
> **For he that is mighty hath done to me great things**; and holy is his name.
> And his mercy is on them that fear him from generation to generation.
> **He hath shewed strength with his arm; he hath scattered the proud in the imagination of their hearts.**
> **He hath put down the mighty from their seats, and exalted them of low degree**.
> He hath filled the hungry with good things; and the rich he hath sent empty away.
> He hath holpen his servant Israel, in remembrance of his mercy;
> As he spake to our fathers, to Abraham, and to his seed for ever. [Mary, the mother of Jesus, magnifies the Lord her Savior.]

These respected Bible characters give us biblical illustrations of humility. Humility is a singular upward focus on God and an acceptance of His estimation of us. When we focus on God as our Master, Father, Creator, and Savior, we begin to see ourselves in a more accurate light. We are nothing compared to Him, but we are also precious in His sight. He estimates us as His precious creations and flawed children who can do nothing apart from Him. When we are so busy looking up at God, we don't have time to think of ourselves in a selfish or prideful way. We can only see ourselves as children and servants of God, in His hands of protection, ownership, and control.

▶ Time to think!

WHAT IS THE BIBLICAL DEFINITION OF HUMILITY?

_____

_____

_____

HOW SHOULD WE VIEW GOD? IN LIGHT OF WHO GOD IS, HOW SHOULD WE THEN VIEW OURSELVES AND OTHERS?

_____

_____

_____

God-Empowered Lives

Now that we have defined humility, we can explore our purpose in humility.

First, God calls us to humility because He wants to empower us to live successfully. In our culture, the words *humility*—as we have just Biblically defined it—and *empowering* don't seem compatible. Yet God's Word provides a very different picture of humility and empowerment. Let's look, for example, at Uzziah's story.

▶ Read

II Chronicles 26:3-5, 7, 15b-21

> Sixteen years old was Uzziah when he began to reign, and he reigned fifty and two years in Jerusalem. His mother's name also was Jecoliah of Jerusalem. And he did that which was right in the sight of the LORD, according to all that his father Amaziah did.

And he sought God in the days of Zechariah, who had understanding in the visions of God: and **as long as he sought the LORD, God made him to prosper.**

And God helped him against the Philistines, and against the Arabians . . .

And his name spread far abroad; **for he was marvelously helped, till he was strong.**
But when he was strong, his heart was lifted up to his destruction: for he transgressed against the LORD his God, and went into the temple of the LORD to burn incense upon the altar of incense.
And Azariah the priest went in after him, and with him fourscore priests of the LORD, that were valiant men:
And they withstood Uzziah the king, and said unto him, It appertaineth not unto thee, Uzziah, to burn incense unto the LORD, but to the priests the sons of Aaron, that are consecrated to burn incense: go out of the sanctuary; for thou hast trespassed; neither shall it be for thine honour from the LORD God.
Then Uzziah was wroth, and had a censer in his hand to burn incense: and while he was wroth with the priests, the leprosy even rose up in his forehead before the priests in the house of the LORD, from beside the incense altar.
And Azariah the chief priest, and all the priests, looked upon him, and, behold, he was leprous in his forehead, and they thrust him out from thence; yea, himself hasted also to go out, because the LORD had smitten him.
And Uzziah the king was a leper unto the day of his death, and dwelt in a several house, being a leper; for he was cut off from the house of the LORD: and Jotham his son was over the king's house, judging the people of the land.

Your Strongest Moment

Uzziah's story presents one of the great paradoxes of the Bible—your strongest moment can actually be your weakest. When Uzziah was young, inexperienced, and aware of those facts, he did what was right, and the Lord gave him success. The verses to follow describe his success with phrases like *"And God helped him . . ."* and *"for he was marvelously helped . . ."*
However, Uzziah's story takes a sad turn in verse 16, beginning with the phrase "**But *when he was strong, his heart was lifted up to his destruction.*"** Uzziah lived an empowered life until he bought into the lie that his power source was *himself*. The moment he forgot his power source, the moment he tried to take the credit and the honor from God, his life spiraled into failure. Uzziah's strongest moment in *himself* was the weakest moment of his life. God removed His power from

Uzziah's life and, as a result, Uzziah lost his health and his kingdom.

You see, God doesn't call us to humility because he wants us to be pitiful or powerless. He calls us to humility because He wants us to be empowered to live the best life possible! While we may not take life into our own hands as drastically as Uzziah did in II Chronicles, sometimes we attempt to do even the smallest things in our own power instead of asking for God's. We are going against God's will when we attempt to take the credit for even the smallest details in our lives. Only when we recognize and confess that anything good that we have and anything good that we are comes from the Heavenly Father are we living fully God-empowered lives!

So, what exactly is a God-empowered life? To empower someone means to give strength or confidence to someone. In politics today, the authority of the Constitution gives people the power to exercise their civil liberties. As American citizens, we are not confident because of our own abilities or authority. Rather, we cannot be trampled on by the government because we appeal to the Constitution's authority. When it comes to the God-empowered life, the authority of God's Word gives us the power to exercise righteous living. We should not be confident in our own abilities, but we can be confident when we appeal to God's authority.

▶ Read

Psalm 138:6
> Though the LORD be high, yet hath he respect unto the lowly: but the proud he knoweth afar off.

Colossians 1:10-11, 16-17
> That ye might walk worthy of the Lord unto all pleasing, being fruitful in every good work, and **increasing in the knowledge of God;**
> **Strengthened with all might, according to his glorious power,** unto all patience and longsuffering with joyfulness;
>
> **For by him** were all things created, that are in heaven, and that are in earth, visible and invisible, whether they be thrones, or dominions, or principalities, or powers: all things were created **by him, and for him:**
> And he is before all things, and by him all things consist.

John 15:5
> I am the vine, ye are the branches: He that abideth in me, and I in him, the same bringeth forth much fruit: for **without me ye can do nothing.**

The Way Up is to Look Up

As we saw earlier in this study, these verses tell us that we are meant to live for God, with God, and by God's power—not our own. As King Uzziah learned, none of us can do right without God's power. In our own power, our good works are worthless and corrupted with selfish motives. When we are smug or satisfied with living life in our own power, we are living on low battery mode. It's like we are living on thirty-percent power and draining fast when all we need to do is plug ourselves into a limitless power source—God Himself. Living a life of self-focus is a recipe for powerlessness and failure. If we constantly look inward to muster up the courage and capability needed to conquer life's challenges, we will always come up short. One day, all our hard work and self-earned success will come crashing down on us, as it did for Uzziah.

In contrast, if we are looking upward and depending on God, we will be fully charged for whatever God gives us to do. As Psalm 138 indicates, *we are closest to God when we are at our lowest.* When we know that we are nothing apart from Him and are dependent on Him for all the good works we are called to, He is close to us.

Although the people at the tower of Babel thought they could climb to God, the Bible teaches that the way up is down. The way to God is through humility. The purpose of humility is not to make us pitiful or to make people believe that we are virtuous. (Isn't that a flip-side of pride?) Our purpose in humility is to live empowered lives for the glory of God! The successful Christian life is all about doing all according to God's will, in God's power, and for God's glory.

▶ **Time to think!**

WHAT DOES IT MEAN TO LIVE A GOD-EMPOWERED LIFE?

_____

_____

_____

ARE THERE ANY AREAS OF YOUR LIFE THAT YOU'VE BEEN TACKLING IN YOUR OWN POWER OR FOR WHICH YOU HAVE BEEN SEEKING TO TAKE THE CREDIT AWAY FROM GOD? IF SO, WRITE A PRAYER TO GOD ASKING FOR HIS FORGIVENESS AND POWER IN YOUR LIFE:

_____

_____

_____

Empowering Others

Not only is humility about empowering our lives, but humility is also about empowering others. Child of God, don't buy into the lie of our culture today that says you have to put down others in order to elevate yourself. This lie has divided humankind for centuries, and it has divided our nation today. Our culture today insists that we have to put down men in order to elevate women. The world demands that we attack people of one ethnicity in order to raise up people of another ethnicity. Modern society claims that you have to shame people of one body type in order to support people with another body type. As Christians, we are called to ditch what society says about humility and self-esteem and instead look to what the Bible says about humility and self-esteem.

▶ Read

Philippians 2:3-10

> Let nothing be done through strife or vainglory; but in lowliness of mind **let each esteem other better than themselves.**
>
> Look not every man on his own things, but every man also on the things of others.
>
> **Let this mind be in you**, which was also in Christ Jesus:
>
> Who, being in the form of God, thought it not robbery to be equal with God:
>
> But made himself of no reputation, and took upon him the form of a servant, and was made in the likeness of men:
>
> And being found in fashion as a man, he humbled himself, and became obedient unto death, even the death of the cross.
>
> **Wherefore God also hath highly exalted him**, and given him a name which is above every name:
>
> That at the name of Jesus every knee should bow, of things in heaven, and things in earth, and things under the earth;

These verses seem to go against every fiber of flawed human nature, and they certainly go against modern society's philosophy. The world does not encourage us to empower others, treat others as better than ourselves, and look after their affairs before we do our own. We have our own problems, right? When we are faced with low self-esteem, self-doubt, and self-hate, the world is happy to assure us with phrases like:

"**You** are enough!"

"Don't let anyone dull **your** shine!"

"You are amazing just the way **you** are!"

"Believe in **yourself**!"

The problem with these sayings is that they make the answer to low self-esteem all about…well…self. The answer to negative self-focus is not positive self-focus. We cannot look within ourselves for the solution to low self-esteem just as we cannot look within ourselves to find the cure for high self-esteem. The answer to low self-esteem is no self-esteem.

Esteem Others

The Bible says that strife is always a result of pride or esteeming ourselves. Philippians 2:3 tells us that we can avoid strife and vainglory through a *"lowliness of mind."* What does it mean when the Bible tells us to *"in lowliness of mind"* esteem others better than ourselves? Well, according to the dictionary, the word esteem means to respect or lift up someone. In that case, we really shouldn't be esteeming ourselves in either direction, low or high. The only One who should be esteemed here is God Himself! Yet when we esteem—or respect and lift up—God above all else, we will esteem other people more than we esteem ourselves. How can we esteem others? Philippians 2:4 answers that question: *"Look not every man on his own things, but every man also on the things of others."* When we put other people's needs and wants before our own, we are esteeming them better than ourselves. The typical reaction to such an against-the-grain command is: Well, if I don't stick up for myself, who will? If I don't esteem myself highly, who will esteem me? God puts that fear to rest in James 4:10: *"Humble yourselves in the sight of the Lord, and he shall lift you up."* When we focus on lifting others up instead of worrying about ourselves, God promises that He will lift us up!

Christ's Example

Our example of esteeming others above self is Jesus Christ. Although He was fully God, Jesus humbled himself in the sight of God the Father and *"became obedient unto death, even the death of the cross"* (Phil. 2:8). He esteemed others above Himself by putting His Father's will and our best interest before His own. Philippians 2:9 says, *"Wherefore God also hath highly exalted him, and given him a name which is above every name."* If Jesus Christ, the Son of God, could esteem others, so can we. Believe God about your worth, treat others with high esteem, and trust that God will lift you up. The answer to high or low self-esteem is to esteem God and others above self.

Esteeming and empowering others means making others stronger and more confident in Christ. Just as God wants us to be strong and confident in Him, God wants to use us to make others strong and confident in Him as well. The Bible provides many examples of Christians who empowered others for living the Christian life. For example, the book of Deuteronomy opens with Moses' farewell address to the people of Israel right before they were about to enter the Promised Land. Let's read a portion of his farewell address in chapter three.

▶ Read

Deuteronomy 3:23-28

> And I besought the LORD at that time, saying,
>
> O Lord GOD, thou hast begun to shew thy servant thy greatness, and thy mighty hand: for what God is there in heaven or in earth, that can do according to thy works, and according to thy might?
>
> I pray thee, let me go over, and see the good land that is beyond Jordan, that goodly mountain, and Lebanon.
>
> But the LORD was wroth with me for your sakes, and would not hear me: and the LORD said unto me, Let it suffice thee; speak no more unto me of this matter.
>
> Get thee up into the top of Pisgah, and lift up thine eyes westward, and northward, and southward, and eastward, and behold it with thine eyes: for thou shalt not go over this Jordan.
>
> But charge Joshua, and **encourage him, and strengthen him:** for he shall go over before this people, and he shall cause them to inherit the land which thou shalt see.

Moses' Example

Perhaps you remember the story in Numbers that tells of Moses' disobedience when he hit the rock instead of speaking to the rock to bring forth water as God had instructed. Because of that rebellious act, God had barred Moses from entering the Promised Land. Here in Deuteronomy chapter three, Moses recounts asking God one more time for permission to enter the Promised Land, but God denies the request. Instead, God tells Moses to fill Joshua up with courage and to strengthen Joshua to be the next leader of Israel.

What could be more humbling than training up a young whipper-snapper to do your job and to receive the blessing that was withheld from you? In the spirit of humility, Moses trained, encouraged, and strengthened Joshua for the job that God had given Joshua. Moses had to put God's will before his own desire to see the Promised Land, and he had to put Israel's best interests before his own. This is what humility is about. Humility is about esteeming God and empowering others to do right also.

When I was a child, my dad would often pray a particular prayer over me and my brothers at breakfast or at bedtime. The prayer went something like this: "Lord, help my kids do right and help them help their friends do right!" Dad was asking God to empower us and to extend that empowerment to our friends. The key to humility is God-esteem and God-focus instead of self-esteem and self-focus. And the *purpose of humility is to live a God-empowered life that empowers others to do right also*. Try humility on for size because, "That looks good on you!"

◗ Time to think!

WOULD YOU CONSIDER YOURSELF TO HAVE A LOW OR HIGH SELF-ESTEEM? WHAT IS THE SOLUTION TO LOW (OR HIGH) SELF-ESTEEM?

_____

_____

_____

BASED ON YOUR PREVIOUS ANSWER, WOULD YOU LIKE TO ASK JESUS TO GIVE YOU HIS MIND ON THE MATTER OF HUMILITY? IF SO, WRITE A PRAYER FOR HUMILITY RIGHT HERE:

_____

_____

_____

WHAT DO THE PHRASES "LOWLINESS OF MIND" AND "ESTEEM OTHER BETTER THAN THEMSELVES" MEAN?

_____

_____

_____

WHAT ARE SOME PRACTICAL WAYS YOU CAN EMPOWER—OR GIVE STRENGTH AND CONFIDENCE TO—OTHERS SO THAT THEY MIGHT DO RIGHT AS WELL?

_____

_____

_____

"God cares for the cast-aways, the thrown away, the discarded of this world"

8 You Are Not Cast Out:
Lessons from Hagar

In Abraham's household lived a young Egyptian woman who felt worthless. She felt worthless because she was worthless. Well, she was worth a few pieces of money but not much else. She was worth the work she could perform for her masters but nothing more. She felt like she was a light-weight, a nothing, a slave…because she was. Hagar was a slave, and she would always be one.

The negative thoughts and self-loathing churned her stomach daily. Every morning, before the sun would wake, Hagar would wake and attempt to shut out her sorrows with a busy mind and busier hands. Yet, as she cleaned and cooked and fetched water, a dark shadow seemed to follow her everywhere—that shadow that engulfed her and wrapped her in depression. Nothing seemed to bring her out from under that shadow until one day—one day, something unexpected happened. Something wonderfully unexpected!

Abraham, her mistress's husband, approached her. He spoke to her, not merely as a slave, but as a woman. He asked her—*her*, Hagar, the bondwoman—to be the mother of his child. Abraham looked her in the eyes and told her that he believed God would bless him with the promised heir through *her!* At that moment, the shadow seemed to scamper away from her and into the corner of the tent like a skittish kitten. She would be like Sarah now—not just a bondwoman, but a wife to Abraham!

Only months later, Hagar put her hand on her belly and thought she could feel another hand meet hers. It was *her* baby—hers and Abraham's child! The shadow that had followed her for so long was nowhere to be found. Hagar basked in the sunshine of attention and care that Abraham ordered for her to have all day, every day. After all, she was no longer just the bondwoman. She carried Abraham's hope, pride, and joy within her. Now, when she saw her mistress, she did not shrivel inside and cower. No, Hagar tilted her chin upward and pierced her mistress with dark eyes. No longer did she see her mistress as a woman who had everything and herself as a light-weight. Now, Hagar was worth more to Abraham than Sarah because Hagar had something Sarah didn't have. Hagar had a child.

The day finally came, and Hagar brought forth a son! Abraham cradled the baby boy in his arms with Hagar and Sarah both watching. For a moment, Abraham glanced up from the baby's red face and locked eyes with Hagar. She thought she caught him smile at her. And she thought Sarah must've noticed, too, because she stormed out of the room.

As the weeks passed, the baby grew. He smiled and giggled and squeezed Abraham's finger. Hagar continued to live in a dream as Abraham continued to care for her and for *their son*, Ishmael. Even Sarah's glares and curt manner could not puncture the bubble that surrounded Hagar these days. The days since Ishmael's birth, Hagar felt she had just as much right, if not more, to Abraham's affection as Sarah did.

Then one day, Sarah did more than just glare

at her. Sarah took out her frustration on Hagar and shattered the dream she'd been living in for months. In a blur of tears, Hagar snatched her baby and fled from the tent of Sarah and Abraham.

Chased by that shadow again, Hagar traveled further into the wilderness where she was sure no one could find her. But there, God found her. And He spoke soothingly to her and promised to care for her and for Ishmael if she would return to Abraham and Sarah. So, Hagar obeyed God. She went back to her master and mistress, and although things could never really be the same as they were before, Hagar did her best to carry on with life as if nothing had happened between her and Abraham.

Then something else changed. Sarah was finally blessed with a child—a son! Now, Abraham no longer considered Hagar's son, Ishmael, to be the child of promise. No longer did Hagar have something that Sarah did not have! Abraham cast out Hagar and Ishmael because they were no longer needed. Once again, the Egyptian bondwoman found herself in the wilderness. Alone again. Worthless again. Cast out.

God Has a Plan for Castaways

As you are reading this story, dear reader, you have most likely not lived the life of a slave. Still, it is possible for you to live under the same shadow as Hagar did. Perhaps the same words have echoed in your ear day after day that you are worthless and good for nothing except what people may get out of you. Maybe you, like Hagar, have searched for worth in something or someone else. That something may not be a child as it was for Hagar, but perhaps it is a possession, a position, or a relationship. Maybe you have swallowed the lie that if you just had that possession, position, or person, then finally you would be worth something. Well, friend, Hagar's story doesn't end in the wilderness. As we follow Hagar's journey in Genesis 21, we can learn some valuable lessons about our worth.

▶ Read

Genesis 21:1-18

> And the LORD visited Sarah as he had said, and the LORD did unto Sarah as he had spoken.
> For Sarah conceived, and bare Abraham a son in his old age, at the set time of which God had spoken to him.
> And Abraham called the name of his son that was born unto him, whom Sarah bare to him, Isaac.
> And Abraham circumcised his son Isaac being eight days old, as God had commanded him.
> And Abraham was an hundred years old, when his son Isaac was born unto him.

And Sarah said, God hath made me to laugh, so that all that hear will laugh with me.

And she said, Who would have said unto Abraham, that Sarah should have given children suck? for I have born him a son in his old age.

And the child grew, and was weaned: and Abraham made a great feast the same day that Isaac was weaned.

And Sarah saw the son of Hagar the Egyptian, which she had born unto Abraham, mocking.

Wherefore she said unto Abraham, **Cast out this bondwoman** and her son: for the son of this bondwoman shall not be heir with my son, even with Isaac.

And the thing was very grievous in Abraham's sight because of his son.

And God said unto Abraham, Let it not be grievous in thy sight because of the lad, and because of thy bondwoman; in all that Sarah hath said unto thee, hearken unto her voice; for in Isaac shall thy seed be called.

And also of the son of the bondwoman will I make a nation, because he is thy seed.

And Abraham rose up early in the morning, and took bread, and a bottle of water, and gave it unto Hagar, putting it on her shoulder, and the child, and sent her away: and she departed, and wandered in the wilderness of Beersheba.

And the water was spent in the bottle, and she cast the child under one of the shrubs.

And she went, and sat her down over against him a good way off, as it were a bowshot: for she said, Let me not see the death of the child. And she sat over against him, and lift up her voice, and wept.

And God heard the voice of the lad; and the angel of God called to Hagar out of heaven, and said unto her, What aileth thee, Hagar? fear not; for **God hath heard** the voice of the lad where he is.

Arise, lift up the lad, and hold him in thine hand; for I will make him a great nation.

In this story, no one seems exempt from hurt. Who was in the right, and who was in the wrong in this story? Who deserved mercy, and who deserved justice? The truth is that everyone—Abraham, Sarah, Hagar, and Ishmael—were in the wrong in this story. Each one of them made a mistake. Sarah pressured Abraham to have a child with Hagar. Abraham followed Sarah's plan and committed fornication. Hagar's heart did a pendulum swing from self-loathing to self-righteousness, and she looked down on Sarah. Ishmael mocked Abraham and Sarah's son Isaac. Everyone in Genesis 21 was at fault…except God.

God had a plan. He had a plan for each player in this story. As we see from this story, God had a plan for Abraham, the father of a great nation, and Sarah, the mother of the promised son. God had a destiny for Isaac, the promised son that would bring that great nation to fruition. Not only did God have a plan for Abraham, Sarah, and Isaac, but God also had a plan for the throw-aways, the castaways. Yes, God had a plan for a bondwoman and her son. He didn't leave them in the wilderness; He saw them and met them where they were in the wilderness.

Perhaps you feel like a throw-away, a castaway. Your story could be similar to Hagar, in that you have suffered some abuse or mistreatment that has left you feeling worthless and in the wilderness. The truth that saved Hagar from despair is the same for you today.

Let's consider three lessens that we can glean from the castaway and the God of the castaways:

First, the God of the castaways is compassionate.

> **Read**

Psalm 27:10
> When my father and my mother forsake me, **then the LORD will take me up.**

Psalm 68:5
> A **father of the fatherless**, and a judge of the widows, is God in his holy habitation.

Psalm 147:3
> **He healeth** the broken in heart, and bindeth up their wounds.

Isaiah 53:3
> He is **despised** and **rejected** of men; a **man of sorrows**, and a**cquainted with grief**: and we hid as it were our faces from him; he was despised, and we esteemed him not.

Hebrews 4:15
> For we have not an high priest which cannot **be touched with the feeling of our infirmities;** but was in all points tempted like as we are, yet without sin.

Whatever your current circumstance, realize that God is with you and that He understands what you are going through. Even if no one else does, the God of the castaways sees you where you are right now, just as He saw Hagar in the wilderness. And just as God showed compassion to Hagar, God cares for you! Amazingly, God Himself knows what it is to be cast out, forgotten, and betrayed. Jesus Christ, God in a body, came to this earth and experienced rejection from his own people and, ultimately, faced death on the behalf of people who did not love Him in return. While He was on this earth, He endured hatred, loneliness, rejection, and separation from God.

The reason God is compassionate toward us is that He can empathize with us. He is touched by the plight of the cast-out. He is the advocate of the oppressed, the widows, the fatherless, and the abused. God knows what every person is going through or ever will go through because He's already been through it. Nothing you face is out of God's comprehension or compassion. Even when no one else understands what you are going through, you can rest in the compassionate God who can empathize with you.

Second, the God of the castaways is capable!

My dad has often asked, "What good would a compassionate God be to you if He were just as incapable of changing your situation as you were?" Let's look at some people and passages that answer that question:

▶ Read

Deuteronomy 31:6 (Spoken to the children of Israel as they were about to enter the Promised Land)
> Be strong and of a good courage, fear not, nor be afraid of them: for the LORD thy God, he it is that doth go with thee; he will not fail thee, nor forsake thee.

II Samuel 22:33 (King David after God delivered him from his enemies)
> God is my strength and power: And he maketh my way perfect.

Psalm 73:25-26 (David the Psalmist)
> Whom have I in heaven but thee? and there is none upon earth that I desire beside thee.
> My flesh and my heart faileth: but God is the strength of my heart, and my portion for ever.

Psalm 138:3, 6-8 (David the Psalmist)
> In the day when I cried thou answerdest me, and strengthenedst me with strength in my soul.
>
> Though the LORD be high, yet hath he respect unto the lowly: but the proud he knoweth afar off.
> Though I walk in the midst of trouble, thou wilt revive me: thou shalt stretch forth thine hand against the wrath of mine enemies, and thy right hand shall save me.

The LORD will perfect that which concerneth me: thy mercy, O LORD, endureth for ever: forsake not the works of thine own hands.

Proverbs 18:10 (King Solomon)
The name of the LORD is a strong tower: the righteous runneth into it, and is safe.

Isaiah 43:16-19 (Prophet Isaiah after the children of Israel had failed again)
Thus saith the LORD, which maketh a way in the sea, and a path in the mighty waters;
Which bringeth forth the chariot and horse, the army and the power; they shall lie down together, they shall not rise: they are extinct, they are quenched as tow.
Remember ye not the former things, neither consider the things of old.
Behold, I will do a new thing; now it shall spring forth; shall ye not know it? I will even make a way in the wilderness, and rivers in the desert.

Jeremiah 50:34 (Prophet Jeremiah after the Babylonian captivity)
Their Redeemer is strong; the LORD of hosts is his name: he shall thoroughly plead their cause, that he may give rest to the land, and disquiet the inhabitants of Babylon.

Just as the Redeemer of Israel, your Redeemer is strong. In fact, you and Israel share the same strong Redeemer! And just as He did for the Israelites so many years ago, He is ready and able to plead the cause of His children.

As these passages indicate, no matter what you are walking through, the God of the castaways is capable of strengthening you to walk with courage. Just as He gave Hagar the strength to take her son and walk back to Abraham and Sarah's household, He will strengthen you to walk the path before you. Even when no one else is there for you, even when your heart is failing, God is the strength of your heart, and He is all you need. No matter what wrongs you have done or what wrongs have been done to you in the past, God is capable of doing a "new thing" in your life. He is known for making ways in the wilderness and rivers in the desert. Just ask Hagar! Or David, for that matter. Or the prophets Isaiah and Jeremiah. If you feel like a castaway, you are in good company. Like the others mentioned here, remember that the God of the castaways is both compassionate *and* capable.

Third, the God of the castaways wants to hear your cry.

We have seen that God is both a compassionate and capable God of the castaways. So how can you tap into God's capability on your behalf?

▶ Read

Psalm 62:5-8

> My soul, wait thou only upon God; for my expectation is from him.
> He only is my rock and my salvation: he is my defence; I shall not be moved.
> In God is my salvation and my glory: the rock of my strength, and my refuge, is in God.
> Trust in him at all times; ye people, **pour out your heart before him**: God is a refuge for us. Selah.

Psalm 63:1-2

> O God, thou art my God; **early will I seek thee**: my soul thirsteth for thee, my flesh longeth for thee in a dry and thirsty land, where no water is;
> To see thy power and thy glory, so as I have seen thee in the sanctuary.

Psalm 88:1-2

> O LORD God of my salvation, **I have cried day and night before thee:**
> Let **my prayer** come before thee: incline thine ear unto my cry;

As these verses direct us, we can pour out our hearts before the Lord and know that He will hear us. Perhaps, like Hagar, you have been wronged by others and put in a hurtful situation. Maybe you have done wrong yourself and feel that you are stuck in a situation that your own sin created. Whatever your situation, God invites you to pour out your heart to Him.

We may not be able to tell anyone else what is burdening our hearts, but we can tell the God of the castaways. We can ask for forgiveness when guilt crushes our spirit. We can ask for peace when trouble swirls around us. We have God's promise that He will never forsake us even when we feel lonely. If God refused to forsake a slave woman and her illegitimate son in the wilderness, He is not any more likely to forsake you. As Hagar did, we can cry out for a way through a trial. As Hagar found, God is known for making a way in the wilderness and rivers in the desert.

If you will lift your eyes off of your circumstances and up to the God of the castaways, you will hear him say, "Behold, I will do a new thing." He did it for Hagar, and He can do it for you, too. Although we humans make mistakes and complicate life, God has a plan for each of us. God had a plan for Hagar just as surely as He did for Isaac. Whether you are feeling cast-out because of sin or situations beyond your control, know that God sees, cares, hears, and has a plan for you.

God is The God of Castaways

Through this beautiful story, God shows us another glimpse of who He is—the God of castaways. People make mistakes, and others are affected by those mistakes. Yet God is bigger than people's complexities. God sees the forgotten, and He hears the silenced. God cares for the cast-aways, the thrown-away, the discarded of this world. He loves the despised, the mocked, and the unlovely. God has a plan for the people who are told that they are mistakes, complicated, or an accident.

In God's eyes, no one is a throw-away or an outcast. Everyone is designed by God, and everyone has the chance to turn to God for help and guidance. For those who are humble enough to seek Him and His way, God will pull them out of their messy life and give them a bright future. Just as Hagar, lost in a dry desert, found God there, we also can find God and His plan for our future when we seek Him.

▶ **Time to think!**

HOW CAN GOD SAY THAT HE UNDERSTANDS WHAT WE ARE GOING THROUGH?

_____

_____

_____

DO YOU FEEL LIKE A CASTAWAY, AND IF SO, WHY?

_____

_____

_____

WHAT CAN WE LEARN FROM HAGAR'S EXPERIENCE? WHAT THREE THINGS SHOULD WE DO WHEN WE FIND OUR SELVES "CAST OUT IN THE WILDERNESS"?

_____

_____

_____

"God will never ask something of you
that He Himself has not already given."

9 "Give Me Your Rice!": Lessons from Abraham

Seven-year-old Billy Simms glanced both ways across the cafeteria before rapidly taking his long legs to his normal lunch table. The lanky boy slid into his seat and double checked to make sure the coast was clear. With a sigh of relief and basking in the solitude, Billy unwrapped his ham sandwich and lifted it to his mouth. Then he heard something that turned his hunger cramps into a thunderstorm in his stomach.

"Hey! What do you think you're doing?" It was the voice of Jim Talon, the second-grade-class bully, and Billy's constant tormenter.

Billy slowly lowered his sandwich back to the table and kept his eyes downcast.

"What do you want?" Billy murmured still staring at his sandwich.

"I want your sandwich."

"Oh." Billy's eyes darted back and forth, searching for an escape route.

"But Jim, if I give you my sandwich, what am I going to eat?"

Jim Talon shrugged and then smirked.

"I dunno. That's your problem, Billy. Now hand it over," Jim said, lowering his tone and shaking his fist in Billy's face.

What God Wants

While God is certainly no bully, has God ever asked for what you felt was too much? Has God ever confused you with what He asks of you? If anyone ever had the right to say "Yes," Abraham would be the one!

In Genesis chapter twelve, God promised to make a great nation of Abraham, through which all the other nations of the earth would be blessed. God promised Abraham in Genesis chapter thirteen that his descendants would be innumerable like the sand of the earth and the stars of the sky. In chapters seventeen and eighteen God again affirmed His covenant with Abraham, stating, *"Is anything too hard for the LORD?"*

Not until Genesis twenty-one did Abraham and Sarah see this promise fulfilled in their son, Isaac. After years of waiting, moments of wondering, and more years of waiting, Abraham received the greatest gift of his life—the gift of the promised heir, through which a great nation would spring and the great Messiah would come. God had come through, just as He promised! Then the joy of Genesis twenty-one turned to the confusion of Genesis twenty-two when God asked something of Abraham that was too great a request. God makes a confusing, baffling, terrifying request of Abraham.

▶ **Read**

Genesis 22:1-3

> And it came to pass after these things, that God did tempt Abraham, and said unto him, Abraham: and he said, Behold, here I am.
> And he said, Take now thy son, thine only son Isaac, whom thou lovest, and get thee into the land of Moriah; and offer him there for a burnt offering upon one of the mountains which I tell thee of.
> And Abraham rose up early in the morning, and saddled his ass, and took two of his young men with him, and Isaac his son, and clave the wood for the burnt offering, and rose up, and went unto the place of which God had told him.

In chapter 22, God asked for a little more from Abraham than his ham sandwich. God asked for Abraham's son, the very son that God Himself had promised to give him! God seemed to contradict His own promise and His own character with this one request.

Surely Abraham felt a mix of emotions—sorrow, fear, confusion—and yet he obeyed. How could Abraham obey a God who seemed to be acting out of character? Abraham had a focus that enabled him to obey a God that asked too much of him.

Who God Is

Let's see how Abraham responded to God's seemingly out-of-character request.

▶ **Read**

Genesis 22:14

> And Abraham called the name of the place Jehovah-jirah: as it is said to this day, In the mount of the LORD it shall be seen.

Hebrews 11:17-19

> By faith Abraham, when he was tried, offered up Isaac: and he that had received the promises offered up his only begotten son.
> Of whom it was said, That in Isaac shall thy seed be called:
> **Accounting that God was able to raise him up**, even from the dead; from whence also he received him in a figure.

Amidst the fear and confusion at God's request, Abraham had faith that God would remain true to His covenant with Abraham. He trusted God's good character, even when God seemed to be acting out of character. Even when Abraham couldn't understand God's request, he trusted God's heart. Abraham believed that God would do whatever it took to keep His promise of Abraham's seed, even if it meant raising Isaac from the dead! Abraham operated on the same assumption that he had made about God back in Genesis 18:25, "*Shall not the Judge of all the earth do right?*"

Like Abraham, when we feel that God is acting out of character or asking too much of us, we must dwell on what we do know about God's heart and character. *We must focus, not on what we think God wants from us, but on Who God is.* Let's look at some aspects of God's character that we should dwell on during trying times:

God is good and merciful.

Psalm 31:19, "O how great is thy goodness, which thou hast laid up for them that fear thee; which thou hast wrought for them that trust in thee before the sons of men!

Psalm 86:15, "But thou, O Lord, art a God full of compassion, and gracious, longsuffering, and plenteous in mercy and truth."

Psalm 116:5, "Gracious is the LORD, and righteous; yea, our God is merciful."

Psalm 119:68, "Thou art good, and doest good; teach me thy statutes."

God is righteous and holy, and He can do no wrong.

Psalm 36:6, "Thy righteousness is like the great mountains; thy judgements are a great deep: O LORD, thou preservest man and beast."

Psalm 71:19, "Thy righteousness also, O God, is very high, who hast done great things: O God, who is like unto thee!"

Psalm 119:137, "Righteous art thou, O LORD, and upright are thy judgements."

Psalm 145:17, "The LORD is righteous in all his ways, and holy in all his works."

God is a defense and protection for his people.

II Samuel 22:32, "For who is God, save the LORD? and who is a rock, save our God?"

Psalm 18:30, "As for God, his way is perfect: the word of the LORD is tried: he is a buckler to all those that trust in him."

Psalm 46:1, "God is our refuge and strength, a very present help in trouble."

Psalm 84:11, "For the LORD God is a sun and shield: the LORD will give grace and glory: no good thing will he withhold from them that walk uprightly."

Psalm 94:22, "But the LORD is my defence; and my God is the rock of my refuge."

Psalm 125:2, "As the mountains are round about Jerusalem, so the LORD is round about his people from henceforth even for ever."

God is loving and kind.
Psalm 36:7, "How excellent is thy lovingkindness, O God! therefore the children of men put their trust under the shadow of thy wings."

Psalm 42:8, "Yet the LORD will command his lovingkindness in the daytime, and in the night his song shall be with me, and my prayer unto the God of my life."

Psalm 69:16, "Hear me, O LORD; for thy lovingkindness is good: turn unto me according to the multitude of thy tender mercies."

Psalm 117:2, "For his merciful kindness is great toward us: and the truth of the LORD endureth for ever. Praise ye the LORD."

Psalm 119:76, "Let, I pray thee, thy merciful kindness be for my comfort, according to thy word unto thy servant."

Psalm 143:8, "Cause me to hear thy lovingkindess in the morning; for in thee do I trust: cause me to know the way wherein I should walk; for I lift up my soul unto thee."

Isaiah 54:10, "For the mountains shall depart, and the hills be removed; but my kindness shall not depart from thee, neither shall the covenant of my peace be removed, saith the LORD that hath mercy on thee."

These passages paint powerful pictures of God's character toward us! Just like the mountains that surround and fortify Jerusalem, God surrounds and fortifies His people. Anything that wants to get to you will have to come through God first! Mountains will move and hills will crumble long before God's love and kindness will leave you! While these character traits may seem hard to reconcile with our circumstances at times, they are more solid than our changing circumstances. Because Abraham understood these solid truths about God's immutable character, he was willing to obey God, no matter what. When we focus on God's immutable character, we can better interpret His working in our lives and better trust His heart for us.

▶ **Time to think!**

WHAT IS SOMETHING THAT GOD HAS DONE OR ASKED OF YOU THAT FRIGHTENS OR CONFUSES YOU? WHAT SHOULD WE DO WHEN WE FEEL THAT GOD IS ACTING OUT OF CHARACTER?

_____

_____

_____

WHAT ARE SOME VERSES FROM THE ABOVE LISTS THAT YOU COULD MEMORIZE TO REMIND YOU OF WHO GOD IS IN TRYING TIMES?

_____

_____

How God Responds

Now let's look at God's response to Abraham's faith.

▶ **Read**

Genesis 22:15-23

And the angel of the LORD called unto Abraham out of heaven the second time,

And said, By myself have I sworn, saith the LORD, for because thou hast done this thing, and hast not withheld thy son, thine only son:

That in blessing I will bless thee, and in multiplying I will multiply thy seed as the stars of heaven, and as the sand which is upon the sea shore; and thy seed shall possess the gate of his enemies;

And in thy seed shall all the nations of the earth be blessed; because thou hast obeyed my voice.

So Abraham returned unto his young men, and they rose up and went together to Beer-sheba; and Abraham dwelt at Beer-sheba.

And it came to pass that after these things, that it was told Abraham, saying,
Behold, Milcah, she hath also born children unto thy brother Nahor;
Huz his firstborn, and Buz his brother, and Kemuel the father of Aram,
And Chesed, and Hazo, and Pildash, and Jidlaph, and Bethuel.
And Bethuel begat Rebekah: these eight Milcah did bear to Nahor, Abraham's brother.

In return for Abraham's willingness to give his most prized possession, God gave Abraham much more than he could've ever given to God. In reality, God didn't take Abraham's only son; God gave Abraham many more sons. As you read, the chapter closes with the birth of Abraham's nephews, and…the birth of someone named, Rebekah. That's right, Rebekah, the one who would grow up to be Isaac's wife. Even though Abraham thought he would have to give up Isaac, God knew that He had a bigger, better plan for Isaac. God was going to fulfill his promise to Abraham by providing a way of escape for Isaac and by providing a wife for Isaac. God was planning to grow Abraham's family, even as Abraham was planning to literally kill any hope of a family at all! If God didn't want Isaac, why did God put Abraham through this drama? What is the purpose of God's asking for sacrifices from His children?

▶ Read

Psalm 51:16-17
> For thou desirest not sacrifice; else would I give it: thou delightest not in burnt offering.
> The sacrifices of God are a broken spirit: a broken and a contrite heart, O God, thou wilt not despise."

Romans 12:1
> I beseech you therefore, brethren, by the mercies of God, that ye present your bodies a living sacrifice, holy, acceptable unto God, which is your reasonable service.

What God Really Wants

At the end of the day, God doesn't want us to sacrifice something for Him. God wants us to offer ourselves as a living sacrifice to Him every day! Abraham's act of willingness to sacrifice his only son and hope was simply a demonstration of the state of Abraham's heart. His heart was one of self-sacrifice to God. Since Abraham viewed his life as coming from God and belonging to God, he was willing to do anything for God in return. At the end of that trying day, Abraham realized that God's purpose in asking was not to take anything from Abraham. Rather, God's purpose in asking was to show Abraham the state of his own heart and to strengthen his faith in God's character. God wanted Abraham's heart, yes. But God knew that when Abraham entrusted his heart to Him, Abraham would gain the gift of a deeper, stronger faith in God's goodness and plan for his life.

That day, did Abraham really give God his son? As we read, God actually provided a ram for the sacrifice in Isaac's stead. God was the One giving that day! And God's giving that day was merely a picture of what He would give one day on a hill called Golgotha. Abraham did not have to sacrifice his only son, but God did give His only Son, Jesus Christ, as a sacrifice for us all.

Romans 8:32 emphasizes the fact that we could never out-give God Himself: "*He that spared not his own Son, but delivered him up for us all, how shall he not with him also freely give us all things?*" In light of this truth, we see that *God will never ask something of you or me that He Himself has not already given.* He will never ask too much of us. He couldn't! God has already given the ultimate—His life in exchange for our eternal salvation. As Romans 12:1 says, it only makes sense to give yourself completely to the One who has given all for you.

▶ Time to think!

WHAT IS THE PURPOSE OF GOD'S ASKING SACRIFICES OF HIS CHILDREN?

_____

_____

_____

WHEN IT SEEMS LIKE GOD IS ASKING TOO MUCH OF US, WHAT IS HE REALLY ASKING FOR?

_____

_____

WHY COULD GOD NEVER ASK TOO MUCH OF US?

We started this chapter with a cafeteria scenario. Poor Billy Simms had to hand over his lunch to the bully, Jim. It was a lot to ask, but fear forced him to give up something very dear to him. As we've seen from Abraham's story, God's dealing with us is much more similar to this next scenario.

The Beggar's Rice

This is a story my dad has told many times during a sermon. Once a long time ago, on a dirt road, crouched a poor beggar man with a little wooden bowl. Every day he would sit by the roadside, begging passersby for something to eat. Too often he went hungry, but one particular day, someone dropped into his little bowl several grains of rice. The beggar cradled his bowl of rice grains and then stuck it out again in hopes that the family of rice grains in his bowl would multiply.

Later that day, a plume of dust billowed up the road and choked the beggar. As he coughed and sputtered, he could also hear something like thunder—hoof-beats on the road. When the dust settled, the beggar's eyes widened to see a magnificent carriage halt in the road right in front of him! A trumpet sounded, a footman opened the carriage door, and out stepped the prince! Immediately, the beggar fell to his face in reverence before the prince.

"Get up," the voice came softly.

The beggar looked side to side, but no one else was in the road except for him. The prince must've been speaking to him! Timidly, he lifted his head and his eyes met the prince's gaze. The prince's eyes seemed to smile at him, and the beggar smiled back. Then came the words that contradicted everything the beggar thought he saw in the prince.

"Give me your rice," commanded the prince.

The beggar's smile melted in shock and sorrow. How could the prince—with a carriage and horses and footmen and the best food in the land—ask for the only thing this beggar had?

"Your majesty, forgive me, but all I have is these few grains of rice. What could you want with them?" His eyes pleaded with the prince.

"Give me your rice," the prince repeated more firmly, extending his hand to the beggar.

"I-I don't understand," the beggar nearly whispered. "This is all I have."

"Give me your rice," demanded the prince a third time. Through tears and with trembling hands, the beggar put his fingers in the bowl and fished out three grains of rice. The prince took the three grains, rolled them around in his palm, and then tossed them to the wind.

The beggar cried out as he watched his three rice grains fly away in the wind. The beggar couldn't help himself. He put his head in his hands and wept. Why must the prince be so cruel to him? Why would he do this? It didn't make sense. Then the prince made another request, another order, really.

"Hold out your hands."

The beggar lifted his head and stared questioningly at the prince. What could he want now, he wondered as he lifted his hands. They were empty hands. Then the beggar watched as the prince reached into his pocket, pulled out his pouch, and counted out three gold coins.

"Here," he said, dropping the three gold coins into the beggar's cupped hands. "One for each grain of rice you gave me." As the beggar stared at his hands in astonishment, the prince turned on his heels, entered his carriage, and was gone before the beggar could think to say anything. As the dust settled and people filled the road again, the beggar could be heard crying, "If only I had given him *all* my rice!"

God Wants You

Surely, none of us want to feel such deep regret as the beggar did because he did not trust the prince completely. Like the prince in the story, sometimes it seems like God is asking too much of us, tormenting us. Yet if we would only surrender our measly grains of rice—all of them—we would find that He has so much more in store for us. God is not like a bully that asks too much of you. God doesn't want your lunch, or your rice, or your only child. God wants you. He wants you to trust Him completely with all of you. Is God saying, "Give me your rice"? Then give it to Him. Give him all of it. He has so much more in store for you.

▶ Time to think!

WHAT IS SOMETHING THAT YOU THINK IS TOO MUCH FOR GOD TO ASK OF YOU? WILL YOU WRITE A PRAYER OF SELF-SACRIFICE TO HIM NOW?

_____

_____

_____

"The next time the Devil preys on your weakness, remember who you are. Remember your inheritance. Don't tap out!"

10 Don't Tap Out: Lessons from Esau

Growing up with two younger brothers has been insightful. Every summer since they were old enough, my brothers have worked and lived up at camp, and since then I've had the inside scoop on what goes on with "the bros" behind closed doors. One of the guys' favorite pastimes in the cabin is a game called "tap-out." Basically, the object of the game is to discover your opponent's weakness and use that to your advantage. In this wrestling match, nothing is off-limits (except maybe biting). In order to win, a player must put his opponent in such an uncomfortable position that he has to "tap-out" in order to be free. The point of the game is to demonstrate your cunning, wrestling skills, and endurance. It's honestly terrifying the lengths some guys will go to avoid being the one who has to tap-out! In Genesis 25, we see two brothers playing what seems like a game of tap-out. Jacob and Esau, twin sons of Isaac and Rebekah, could not have been more different from each other. Esau was a daddy's boy who loved hunting and all things outdoors, while Jacob was a mamma's boy who loved cooking and sticking around the house. Another pastime of Jacob's seemed to be scheming. Jacob was quite the intellectual, and while Esau may have had the advantage physically in this round of tap-out, Jacob knew just the right moves to make in order to put his opponent in a tough spot.

▶ Read

Genesis 25:27-34

> And the boys grew: and Esau was a cunning hunter, a man of the field; and Jacob was a plain man, dwelling in tents.
> And Isaac loved Esau, because he did eat of his venison: but Rebekah loved Jacob.
> And Jacob sod pottage: and Esau came from the field, and he was faint:
> And Esau said to Jacob, Feed me, I pray thee, with that same red pottage; for I am faint: therefore was his name called Edom.
> And Jacob said, Sell me this day thy birthright.
> And Esau said, Behold, I am at the point to die: and what profit shall this birthright do to me?
> And Jacob said, Swear to me this day; and he sware unto him: and he sold his birthright unto Jacob.
> Then Jacob gave Esau bread and pottage of lentils; and he did eat and drink, and rose up, and went his way: thus Esau despised his birthright."

After a long day in the field, overheated and faint, Esau found his twin, Jacob, preparing soup and bread. In desperate hunger, Esau begged Jacob for the food. Knowing that he had Esau just where he wanted him, Jacob made a deal with his brother: Esau's birthright for a good meal. Without hesitation, Esau agreed. In desperation and urgency, he tapped out.

You Have a Birthright

Did you know, dear Christian, that you and I have a birthright? No, you don't live in the Middle Eastern culture of Isaac's day, when the firstborn was given a birthright to the family estate. But like Esau, you have a received a precious birthright, an inheritance, from your Heavenly Father.

▶ Read

Ephesians 1:11-23

> **In whom also we have obtained an inheritance**, being predestinated according to the purpose of him who worketh all things after the counsel of his own will:
> That we should be to the praise of his glory, who first trusted in Christ.
> In whom ye also trusted, after that ye heard the word of truth, the gospel of your salvation: in whom also after that ye believed, ye were sealed with that Holy Spirit of promise,
> Which is the earnest of our inheritance until the redemption of the purchased possession, unto the praise of his glory.
> Wherefore I also, after I heard of your faith in the Lord Jesus, and love unto all the saints,
> Cease not to give thanks for you, making mention of you in my prayers;
> That the God of our Lord Jesus Christ, the Father of glory, may give unto you the spirit of wisdom and revelation in the knowledge of him.
> The eyes of your understanding being enlightened; that ye may know what is the hope of his calling, and what the riches of the glory of his inheritance in the saints,
> And what is the exceeding greatness of his power to us-ward who believe, according to the working of his mighty power,
> Which he wrought in Christ, when he raised him from the dead, and set him at his own right hand in the heavenly places,
> Far above all principality, and power, and might, and dominion, and every name that is named, not only in this world, but also in that which is to come:
> And hath put all things under his feet, and gave him to be the head over all

things to the church,
Which is his body, the fulness of him that filleth all in all.

Colossians 1:10-13
> That ye might walk worthy of the Lord unto all pleasing, being fruitful in every good work, and increasing in the knowledge of God;
> Strengthened with all might, according to his glorious power, unto all patience and longsuffering with joyfulness;
> Giving thanks unto the Father, which hath made us meet to be partakers of the inheritance of the saints in light:
> Who hath delivered us from the power of darkness, and hath translated us into the kingdom of his dear Son:

From these passages, we see that our inheritance as children of God is the power to live a victorious Christian life. We have been delivered from darkness in order to live a brilliant Christian life. However, you do have the option of giving up your birthright for something you perceive as better. Perhaps you are thinking, *What in the world would a Christian perceive as better than victory from sin*?! Well, just like Jacob did, the Devil knows his opponent's weakness. He knows what can make us tap-out and give up our birthright of a victorious Christian life. What is it that drove Esau to a point of desperation, and what could drive us to tap-out as well?

▶ Read

James 1:14-15
> But every man is tempted, when he is drawn away of his own lust, and enticed.
> Then when lust hath conceived, it bringeth forth sin: and sin, when it is finished, bringeth forth death.

Contrary to what we may like to think, temptation does not come out of nothing. When Esau was tempted of Jacob to sell his birthright, that temptation didn't work because of Jacob's cunning. It worked because of Esau's lust. Esau was drawn away and enticed by his own desire for food. Lust, which simply means strong desire or passion, can drive any of us to desperation. While it may be different for each of us, the Devil knows what desire can distract us and make us feel urgently in need. He is aware of what passion we obsess over, even if we are not. Once he can dangle that thing in front of us and put us in an uncomfortable position, the Devil hopes to make us tap-out. He wants us to give up our inheritance of the victorious Christian life for the momentary relief or pleasure of something else. However, God has another purpose for our lives.

Yield to the Spirit

▶ Read

Galatians 5:24-26
> And they that are Christ's have crucified the flesh with the affections and lusts.
> If we live in the Spirit, let us also walk in the Spirit.
> Let us not be desirous of vain glory, provoking one another, envying one another.

Romans 13:13-14
> Let us walk honestly, as in the day; not in rioting and drunkenness, not in chambering and wantonness, not in strife and envying.
> But put ye on the Lord Jesus Christ, and make not provision for the flesh, to fulfill the lusts thereof.

The sins of rioting and drunkenness do not happen overnight. They creep up on those who are distracted by their own desires, obsessing over their own passions. In a moment of desperation, those who are ruled by their own "affections and lusts" (Galatians 5:24) will be ready to tap-out. In contrast, God's purpose for us when we are under the pressure of temptation is to yield our desires and passions to the Holy Spirit. We need to bridle our passions and desires with the reign of God's Holy Spirit. The Spirit produces such fruits as meekness and temperance. Esau certainly wasn't displaying these fruits when he traded his birthright for a meal. If we want to avoid Esau's foolishness, we must ask God's Spirit to reign over our passions and to enable us to be in subjection to God.

▶ Read

James 1:16-17
> Do not err, my beloved brethren.
> Every good gift and every perfect gift is from above, and cometh down from the Father of lights, with whom is no variableness, neither shadow of turning.

Don't Be Deceived

The Devil is the King of false-advertisement. He knows what might tempt us, and he uses counterfeit goods to make us believe that he can satisfy our desires. A practical step toward protection from the Devil's deal-making is to evaluate some of our worst decisions made in our most desperate moments. What desire was at the core of that temptation? In Esau's case, his appetite made him desperate enough to make a decision that would cause him even more conflict in the future.

What is it in our lives that makes us feel the pangs of desperation, urgency, or obsession? Is there an unrestrained hunger for food, wealth, love, popularity, beauty, or possessions? Maybe there's an obsession over movies, books, music, fashion, or sports. Whatever it is, starve yourself of that thing. Do not continue to take in a steady diet of that influence, feeding that desire for more. Whatever unrestrained passion drives us to desperation, urgency, or obsession, that passion makes us vulnerable to the Devil's deal-making. And whenever the Devil makes a deal, he always steals more from you than he gives to you.

Although the Devil dangles counterfeits in front of our faces to make us tap-out, God is the Giver of every good gift. When we surrender our desires to Him, we will never be disappointed. In order to keep the birthright of victory, we must surrender our passions to God's restraint, God's will, and God's timing. So, before the Devil can get you in a head-lock, be aware of the desire that could drive you to desperation. Starve yourself of whatever influences feed that desire or passion. The next time the Devil preys on your weakness, remember who you are. Remember your inheritance.

Don't tap out!

▶ Time to think!

IF TEMPTATION DOES NOT COME OUT OF NOTHING, WHAT IS IT THAT DRIVES US TO DESPERATION, TO A POINT OF TAPPING-OUT?

_____

_____

_____

WHAT IS A DESIRE OR PASSION THAT CAN BECOME A POINT OF TEMPTATION FOR YOU?

_____

_____

_____

WHAT IS GOD'S PURPOSE FOR US WHEN WE ARE UNDER THE PRESSURE OF TEMPTATION?

_____

_____

_____

WHAT IS A PRACTICAL STEP YOU CAN TAKE TO PROTECT YOURSELF FROM BEING VULNERABLE TO THE DEVIL'S DEAL-MAKING?

_____

_____

_____

NOTES

"If you are hungry, dear soul, go get more of God."

11 Recovering from Christian Agnosticism:
Lessons from Jacob

Is it possible for a Christian to live like an agnostic? In other words, is it possible for a Christian to believe God about salvation but then live his or her life as if God doesn't exist, as if He doesn't have a plan and purpose for his or her life? Yes, yes, it is. And the reason I know this is because I'm a Christian who has lived like an agnostic before. Let me explain.

One semester in college I was taking a philosophy class called Christian Evidences. The assignments stimulated my mind and intrigued my intellectual side. I loved working through the arguments against God's existence and uncovering the logical evidence for God's existence. The information was mind-blowing and made so much sense at the same time. Yet, that same semester, I found myself frustrated and in tears about a particular area of my life. I felt like I had no purpose and no future ahead of me, so why not quit right now? All my hard work to chase after my dreams wasn't working out because I was being thwarted, it seemed, at every turn! Then it hit me—oh, the irony that while I was interested in learning about cosmological, teleological, and moral evidences for God's existence, I refused to see God's existence in my own personal life. Yes, I believed that God was real, but I couldn't see Him as real in my own life. I refused to pray about this particular area because I didn't believe God would care, hear, or answer. I had swallowed the idea that God had no purpose for me beyond salvation and that it was up to me to create my own life plan. *Maybe God has a plan, maybe He doesn't*, I thought. Whether or not God had a plan for my life was *unknowable*.

This pill I had swallowed was beginning to show up in my daily functions. My decisions reflected a self-dependent, pull-yourself-up-by-the-boot-straps, make-life-happen mentality. And this mentality caused an avalanche of unnecessary stress, anxiety, and hopelessness. Thoughts like, *I will never be satisfied unless … or If only I could be enough for … and I will finally be at peace if …* plagued me on a daily basis.

At the end of that semester, despite all the wonderful, intellectual arguments I could make for God's existence, I could not see Him anywhere in my life. I finished that semester with a stimulated mind but was left with an exhausted soul. As I wrestled with whether or not God was real in my personal life, I was living as a Christian agnostic.

When the new year rolled around, I began my devotional Bible reading in the book of Genesis, searching for a personal God. That's when I found that I was not alone in this struggle of self-dependence because Jacob struggled with it, too. You may know Jacob as the trickster, deceiver, conniver, and manipulator whom we discussed in a previous chapter of this book. In Genesis chapter 27, we see the reason for Jacob's deceptive and manipulative character.

> **Read**
>
> Genesis 27

Stealing his brother's birthright was not enough for Jacob. He needed more. Jacob's next objective was to trick his father into giving him the blessing as well! Jacob was determined to make life happen the way he wanted it. Perhaps Jacob thought, *Maybe God's plan is for me to have the birthright, maybe it's not. Either way, I have to make it happen or else I will be miserable!* Oh, Jacob worked hard for what he wanted. And he got it, too—he got his father's blessing in his own way. Finally, Jacob experienced the peace he wanted, right? Well, by the end of the chapter Jacob was running for his life because his angry brother wanted to kill him in revenge! Perhaps that is not the peaceful result Jacob wanted. Still, Jacob's story didn't end there.

> **Read**
>
> Genesis 28

A Deal or A Promise

In Genesis 28, we find Jacob in a place called Beer-sheba where he is attempting to rest for the night. That night, he meets God in a dream, and God reassures Jacob of His plan for His life. God is not surprised by Jacob's death-grip on life! Rather God comforts the restless wanderer with these words: "*I am with thee . . . until I have done that which I have spoken to thee of*" (Genesis 28:15). After that, Jacob wakes up and seems to . . . make a deal with God! In verse 20-22, Jacob vows: "*If God will be with me, and will keep me in this way that I go, and will give me bread to eat, and raiment to put on, So that I come again to my father's house in peace; then shall the LORD be my God: And this stone, which I have set for a pillar, shall be God's house: and of all that thou shalt give me I will surely give the tenth unto thee.*" Even while Jacob was attempting to be generous with God, he put several conditional statements in that vow. Jacob vowed to give God a tenth of all that God had given him if God would bless him. While it is never wrong to ask God for what we want or need, we should never condition our dependence on what God will do for us. Any condition we put on our dependence on God is making a deal with God—not making a promise to God. This type of deal-making with God is like saying, "Ok, I know I should trust God, *but in case He doesn't come through for me, I need to have a backup plan.* So God, if you make sure I have food and clothes and stuff, then I will totally obey You! I'll even give you a tenth of my stuff . . . that You gave me!" Trying to make life happen our way is too often a part of who we are. We know that this was certainly a part of who Jacob was as he later wrestled with the Angel of LORD, demanding that He bless him. Jacob experienced that exhaustion of the soul. He wrestled with it (no pun intended) his whole life so that when he stood before Pharaoh at the end of his life, he described his days as "*few and evil*" (Genesis 47:9). Life just never went right for Jacob. This was not because he was purposeless or hopeless. It was not because he didn't work hard enough. The reason Jacob considered his days to be "few and evil" was that *he never came to a point where he consistently believed that God was real in <u>his personal life</u>*. He continued to wrestle with God and never consistently depended on God to make life happen for him.

God's Presence and Plan

This "Christian agnosticism" does not have to define our lives. We can have peace, purpose, and rest in our souls if we will consistently choose to believe in God's literal presence and perfect plan in our lives. Here are some truths to aid us in recovering from Christian agnosticism:

1. God places great value on your life and knows you to your core. Matthew 10:29-31 says, "*Are not two sparrows sold for a farthing? and one of them shall not fall on the ground without your Father. But the very hairs of your head are all numbered. Fear ye not therefore, ye are of more value than many sparrows.*" Look, if God cares about birds, don't think for a silly second that He doesn't care about you–a life He created in His image!

2. God has a plan; it's a good plan, and you can know it. Jeremiah 29:11,13 says, "*For I know the thoughts that I think toward you, saith the LORD, thoughts of peace, and not of evil, to give you an expected end…And ye shall seek me, and find me, when ye shall search for me with all your heart.*" Seek and you will find. And to seek, by definition, means to look and keep looking. When you're looking for your misplaced phone, you don't peek under the couch once and then assume it just cannot be found. No, you look, believing you will find it, and you keep looking until you do find it. Likewise, don't give up so quickly when it comes to seeking God's direction in your life! Just because God hasn't written your destiny in the stars doesn't mean He doesn't have a plan. Keep up the treasure hunt!

3. God responds to BIG, bold, specific, and consistent prayers. I John 5:14,15 says, "*And this is the confidence that we have in him, that, if we ask any thing according to his will, he heareth us: And if we know that he hear us, whatsoever we ask, we know that we have the petitions that we desired of him.*" Of course, we can't expect to see God's hand in our lives if we have become so faithless that we've stopped asking

God for things! We don't need much faith to start praying. Praying is "faithing." And asking according to His will means that we ask for what we want/need boldly, specifically, and consistently, while also holding it up to Him saying, "not my will, but thine be done. I trust You and Your choices for my life." God says when we pray like this, our desires begin to match His and then we "have the petitions that we desire of him."

4. God truly satisfies. Psalm 107:8-9 says, "*Oh, that men would praise the LORD for his goodness, and for his wonderful works to the children of men! For he satisfieth the longing soul, and filleth the hungry soul with goodness.*" Don't believe the lie that "if only" you have that thing, career, person, or place, then you would be at peace, satisfied, and happy. Only God can do that. So if you are hungry, dear soul, go get more of God. Learn more about Him. Talk to Him about everything so much more than you already do. He is good, and He will fill you up with that goodness! We were created so that only God-worship can satisfy our souls.

5. Jesus died for you. II Corinthians 5:14-15 says, "*For the love of Christ constraineth us; because we thus judge, that if one died for all, then were all dead: And that he died for all, that they which live should not henceforth live unto themselves, but unto him which died for them, and rose again.*" Ok. If God Almighty could confine Himself to a body, confine Himself to human limits such as fatigue, hunger, and pain, and then could die an agonizing death in our place, don't you think we could just live for Him? If we could trust Jesus to save our souls, why do we find it so so hard to trust Him with our earthly mission? Jesus did what was best for your soul even though it cost Him more than we could imagine. We wouldn't have a life if it weren't for Jesus! And He didn't go through the agony of the cross just so you could accept His free gift of salvation and then live the rest of your life as if He doesn't exist! He did it so that you could live the best life possible–so you could live Christ's life.

So . . . when will you come to the realization that you cannot make life happen? When will you stop wandering and find your home in God's will for you right now? When will you surrender your restlessness to His rest? When will you stop looking out for "number one" and start looking to the One for your hope, joy, worth, identity, peace, and life? My prayer is that it doesn't take you as long as it took Jacob. Believe the God who is real in your life!

◗ Time to think!

HOW IS IT POSSIBLE FOR A CHRISTIAN TO LIVE AS AN AGNOSTIC?

_____

_____

_____

WHAT ARE SOME CONDITIONS THAT YOU HAVE PLACED ON YOUR DEPENDENCE ON GOD TO "MAKE LIFE HAPPEN"?

_____

_____

_____

WHAT ARE SOME TRUTHS TO MEDITATE ON THAT WILL HELP YOU TO RECOVER FROM "CHRISTIAN AGNOSTICISM"?

_____

_____

_____

"The story is all about God, and like Joseph,
we are just privileged to be a part of it"

12 Choosing Success Over Self-Pity: Lessons from Joseph

Betrayed, falsely accused, wrongly punished, forgotten—this was his life experience. The people who were supposed to love him the most had betrayed him to slave merchants. The person who had said she loved him had falsely accused him of a crime. The master who had trusted him and given him a high position turned on him, punishing him for a crime he never committed. And the one friend he thought he had left—that friend had forgotten him. That was Joseph's life experience until he was in his early thirties. For a moment, let us pretend that we have never heard the ending of Joseph's story. Imagine that what was just described is the only biography we have on Joseph. If anyone had a reason to cave to self-pity, wouldn't it be someone who was betrayed by his own brothers when his life was only beginning? If anyone had a reason to cry for their losses, wouldn't it be someone who had done right only to be punished for it? If anyone had a reason to be lulled into depressive sleep, wouldn't it be someone whose friends had left him to be perhaps forever forgotten in a prison? Even though Joseph had been wronged by every other person in life, from his brothers to his friends, Joseph did not cave to self-pity or depression.

The End of the Story

Now, remember that you do know the end of the Joseph's story. What word comes to mind when you remember Joseph? Is he a man of success or self-pity? If you consider Joseph to be one of your favorite Bible characters, as I do, you certainly do not picture Joseph as a pitiful person. When you think of Joseph, you think of a successful man, second in command of all Egypt, who single-handedly saved a nation from starvation. And you would be partially correct. Joseph was successful, but not singlehandedly. You and I can be every bit as successful as Joseph was if we learn three lessons from Joseph's life. Joseph's formula for choosing success over self-pity was his passion for God, his purpose from God, and His perspective on God. Let's look at each in turn.

I. Passion for God.

> **▶ Read**
> Genesis 39:7-12
> And it came to pass after these things, that his master's wife cast her eyes

upon Joseph; and she said, Lie with me.

But he refused, and said unto his master's wife, Behold my master wotteth not what is with me in the house, and he hath committed all that he hath to my hand;

There is none greater in this house than I; neither hath he kept back any thing from me but thee, because thou art his wife: how then can I do this great wickedness, and sin against God?

And it came to pass, as she spake to Joseph day by day, that he hearkened not unto her, to lie by her, or to be with her.

And it came to pass about this time, that Joseph went into the house to do his business; and there was none of the men of the house there within.

And she caught him by his garment, saying, Lie with me: and he left his garment in her hand, and fled, and got him out.

The one good thing that had come out of Joseph's being sold into slavery was his position in Potiphar's house. Since Joseph had proven himself a *"prosperous man"* (Genesis 39:2), Potiphar had entrusted him with everything in his household. Then one day Potiphar's wife approached Joseph with a proposition. He refused, but day after day she tempted him. One day, they were alone in the house. None of the men of the house were there. No one would have to know. But still Joseph refused.

How could a young man like Joseph, tempted day after day with no one to keep him accountable, choose to do right every single time? The answer is found in his reply, "How then can I do this great wickedness, and sin against God?" Joseph's reply to her proposition was not rooted in the fear of man. After all, none of the men of the house were there. Potiphar would never have to know. His family would never know or care. In fact, just the chapter before, Joseph's brother Judah had committed adultery! What was to keep Joseph from such sins when he lived in a foreign, pagan country where no one promoted righteousness? Why would Joseph not indulge when he rarely had the opportunity to please himself?

Joseph resisted temptation and remained pure because his passion for God outweighed every other passion in his life. Joseph recognized that God was with him, whether in his homeland or in a pagan land. Joseph's desire to please God was stronger than his desire to please himself.

Like Joseph, we will only be as strong as our passion for God. Our passion for God is evident in the little choices we make every day. Do we choose to have our devotional time with God or do we put it off until we run out of time at the end of the day? Is prayer our first response to a problem, or do we seek out other people or plans to ease our stress? When no one else is in the room, when it's just you and the temptation, neither the fear of man nor the passion for pleasure will keep you from sin. In our most trying moments, only a preeminent passion for God and an awareness of His presence like Joseph had will keep us pure.

▶ Read

Psalm 1:1-2

> Blessed is the man that walketh not in the counsel of the ungodly, nor standeth in the way of sinners, nor sitteth in the seat of the scornful.
> But his delight is in the law of the LORD; and in his law doeth he meditate day and night.

Paslm 73:23-25

> Nevertheless I am continually with thee: thou hast holden me by my right hand.
> Thou shalt guide me with thy counsel, and afterward receive me to glory.
> Whom have I in heaven but thee? and there is none upon earth that I desire beside thee.

Proverbs 29:25

> The fear of man bringeth a snare: but whoso putteth his trust in the LORD shall be safe.

▶ Time to think!

HOW COULD JOSEPH RESIST TEMPTATION AND REMAIN PURE?

_____

_____

_____

IS THERE A PASSION THAT SUPERSEDES YOUR PASSION FOR GOD CURRENTLY? IF SO, WHY NOT WRITE A PRAYER FOR GOD TO INCREASE YOUR LOVE FOR HIM?

_____

_____

_____

II. Purpose from God.

▶ Read

Genesis 39:20-23

> And Joseph's master took him, and put him into the prison, a place where the king's prisoners were bound: and he was there in the prison.
> But the LORD was with Joseph, and shewed him mercy, and gave him favour in the sight of the keeper of the prison.
> And the keeper of the prison committed to Joseph's hand all the prisoners that were in the prison; and whatsoever they did there, he was the doer of it.
> The keeper of the prison looked not to any thing that was under his hand; because the LORD was with him, and that which he did, the LORD made it to prosper.

Genesis 40:1-8, 14-15, 23

> And it came to pass after these things, that the butler of the king of Egypt and his baker had offended their lord the king of Egypt.
> And Pharaoh was wroth against two of his officers, against the chief of the butlers, and against the chief of the bakers.
> And he put them in ward in the house of the captain of the guard, into the prison, the place where Joseph was bound.
> And the captain of the guard charged Joseph with them, and he served them: and they continued a season in ward.
> And they dreamed a dream both of them, each man his dream in one night, each man according to the interpretation of his dream, the butler and the baker of the king of Egypt, which were bound in the prison.
> And Joseph came in unto them in the morning, and looked upon them, and, behold, they were sad.
> And he asked Pharaoh's officers that were with him in the ward of his lord's house, saying, Wherefore look ye so sadly to day?
> And they said unto him, We have dreamed a dream, and there is no interpreter of it. And Joseph said unto them, Do not interpretations belong to God? tell me them, I pray you.
>
> But think on me when it shall be well with thee, and shew kindness, I pray thee, unto me, and make mention of me unto Pharaoh, and bring me out of this house:

For indeed I was stolen away out of the land of the Hebrews: and here also have I done nothing that they should put me into the dungeon.

Yet did not the chief butler remember Joseph, but forgat him.

Give Good

The last thing on my mind after being wrongfully thrown in prison would be other people. However, Joseph obviously did not spend all of his days pouting in the corner. The Bible says that the keeper of the prison favored Joseph so much that he put Joseph in charge of the prison. Surely, the keeper of the prison would not place a surly, sour-faced prisoner in charge. Another clue that Joseph was not self-centered is found in Genesis 40 when he asks the butler and the baker about their sadness. A self-absorbed person throwing a pity-party would not be able to notice two other random prisoners, but Joseph did.

Even in the prison, Joseph experienced success over self-pity because he recognized his purpose from God. Joseph recognized that God's purpose was not necessarily to give good things to him, but to give good things through him. Rather than sulking and waiting for God to do something good in his life, Joseph actively sought to give good to others. He was so good to the keeper of the prison that he was placed in charge. He was so good to the butler and the baker that he was… forgotten?! Well, Joseph's story doesn't end there. As Joseph allowed God to give good through him to others, Joseph set himself up to get good from God's hand as well.

▶ Read

Genesis 41:1-16, 37-39

> And it came to pass at the end of two full years, that Pharaoh dreamed: and, behold, he stood by the river.
> And, behold, there came up out of the river seven well favoured kine and fatfleshed; and they fed in a meadow.
> And, behold, seven other kine came up after them out of the river, ill favoured and leanfleshed; and stood by the other kine upon the brink of the river.
> And the ill favoured and leanfleshed kine did eat up the seven well favoured and fat kine. So Pharaoh awoke.
> And he slept and dreamed the second time: and, behold, seven ears of corn came up upon one stalk, rank and good.
> And, behold, seven thin ears and blasted with the east wind sprung up after them.
> And the seven thin ears devoured the seven rank and full ears. And Pharaoh

awoke, and, behold, it was a dream.

And it came to pass in the morning that his spirit was troubled; and he sent and called for all the magicians of Egypt, and all the wise men thereof: and Pharaoh told them his dream; but there was none that could interpret them unto Pharaoh.

Then spake the chief butler unto Pharaoh, saying, I do remember my faults this day:

Pharaoh was wroth with his servants, and put me in ward in the captain of the guard's house, both me and the chief baker:

And we dreamed a dream in one night, I and he; we dreamed each man according to the interpretation of his dream.

And there was there with us a young man, an Hebrew, servant to the captain of the guard; and we told him, and he interpreted to us our dreams; to each man according to his dream he did interpret.

And it came to pass, as he interpreted to us, so it was; me he restored unto mine office, and him he hanged.

Then Pharaoh sent and called Joseph, and they brought him hastily out of the dungeon: and he shaved himself, and changed his raiment, and came in unto Pharaoh.

And Pharaoh said unto Joseph, I have dreamed a dream, and there is none that can interpret it: and I have heard say of thee, that thou canst understand a dream to interpret it.

And Joseph answered Pharaoh, saying, It is not in me: God shall give Pharaoh an answer of peace.

And the thing was good in the eyes of Pharaoh, and in the eyes of all his servants.

And Pharaoh said unto his servants, Can we find such a one as this is, a man in whom the Spirit of God is?

And Pharaoh said unto Joseph, Forasmuch as God hath shewed thee all this, there is none so discreet and wise as thou art:

Get Good

In these verses, we see that Joseph's intention was not to get recognition or praise from Pharaoh. Rather, Joseph credited God with the good that he was able to give Pharaoh. In response to Joseph's giving spirit, God rewarded him with something good—a promotion!

Like Joseph, we can overcome self-pity when we realize that *our purpose is not always to get good from God, but to let God give good through us to others.* Perhaps you find yourself in a trial that feels meaningless and painful. No good seems to be coming your way. Instead of praying only for good things from God, pray also for God to give good things through you to others. Your trial may place you in a unique situation to relate to or reach another person that no one else can relate to or reach. When you realize that even in the prison you have so much to give to others, you will find purpose in the pain. And when you pursue that purpose of giving good—not just getting good—you will not go unnoticed. You will find God-given success. Joseph's outcome, and ours too if we follow Joseph's example, can be described by Psalm 37.

◗ Read

Psalm 37:7-27

Rest in the Lord, and wait patiently for him: fret not thyself because of him who prospereth in his way, because of the man who bringeth wicked devices to pass.
Cease from anger, and forsake wrath: fret not thyself in any wise to do evil.
For evildoers shall be cut off: but those that wait upon the LORD, they shall inherit the earth.
For yet a little while, and the wicked shall not be: yea, thou shalt diligently consider his place, and it shall not be.
But the meek shall inherit the earth; and shall delight themselves in the abundance of peace.
The wicked plotteth against the just, and gnasheth upon him with his teeth.
The Lord shall laugh at him: for he seeth that his day is coming.
The wicked have drawn out the sword, and have bent their bow, to cast down the poor and needy, and to slay such as be of upright conversation.
Their sword shall enter into their own heart, and their bows shall be broken.
A little that a righteous man hath is better than the riches of many wicked.
For the arms of the wicked shall be broken: but the LORD upholdeth the righteous.
The LORD knoweth the days of the upright: and their inheritance shall be for ever.
They shall not be ashamed in the evil time: and in the days of famine they shall be satisfied.
But the wicked shall perish, and the enemies of the LORD shall be as the fat of lambs: they shall consume; into smoke shall they consume away.
The wicked borroweth, and payeth not again: but the righteous sheweth mercy, and giveth.
For such as be blessed of him shall inherit the earth; and they that be cursed of him shall be cut off.
The steps of a good man are ordered by the LORD: and he delighteth in his way.

Though he fall, he shall not be utterly cast down: for the LORD upholdeth him with his hand.

I have been young, and now am old; yet have I not seen the righteous forsaken, nor his seed begging bread.

He is ever merciful, and lendeth; and his seed is blessed.

Depart from evil, and do good; and dwell for evermore.

▶ Time to think!

WHAT WAS GOD'S PURPOSE FOR JOSEPH IN THE PRISON?

___

___

___

HOW COULD JOSEPH EXPERIENCE SUCCESS OVER SELF-PITY IN THE PRISON AND BEFORE PHARAOH?

___

___

___

IS THERE A PARTICULAR TRIAL THAT IS TEMPTING YOU TO FEEL SELF-PITY? IF SO, WHY NOT WRITE A PRAYER OF SURRENDER TO GOD AND ASK HIM TO HELP YOU SEE SOMEONE YOU CAN GIVE TO THROUGH THIS?

___

___

___

III. Perspective on God.

▶ **Read**

Genesis 45:4-8

> And Joseph said unto his brethren, Come near to me, I pray you. And they came near. And he said, I am Joseph your brother, whom ye sold into Egypt. Now therefore be not grieved, nor angry with yourselves, that ye sold me hither: **for God did send** me before you to preserve life.
>
> For these two years hath the famine been in the land: and yet there are five years, in the which there shall neither be earing nor harvest.
>
> **And God sent me** before you to preserve you a posterity in the earth, and to save your lives by a great deliverance.
>
> So now it was not you that sent me hither, **but God**: and he hath made me a father to Pharaoh, and lord of all his house, and a ruler throughout all the land of Egypt.

Genesis 50:15-21

> And when Joseph's brethren saw that their father was dead, they said, Joseph will peradventure hate us, and will certainly requite us all the evil which we did unto him.
>
> And they sent a messenger unto Joseph, saying, Thy father did command before he died, saying,
>
> So shall ye say unto Joseph, Forgive, I pray thee now, the trespass of thy brethren, and their sin; for they did unto thee evil: and now, we pray thee, forgive the trespass of the servants of the God of thy father. And Joseph wept when they spake unto him.
>
> And his brethren also went and fell down before his face; and they said, Behold, we be thy servants.
>
> And Joseph said unto them, Fear not: for **am I in the place of God?**
>
> But as for you, ye thought evil against me; **but God meant it unto good,** to bring to pass, as it is this day, to save much people alive.
>
> Now therefore fear ye not: I will nourish you, and your little ones. And he comforted them, and spake kindly unto them.

Who is in Control?

Finally, the day had come. An ironic twist of events had placed the brothers who had betrayed Joseph at his very mercy. Joseph had the power to choose life or death, mercy or revenge, for the brothers who had catapulted him into this roller-coaster ride of life. But what did Joseph choose when this day finally came? Joseph forgave them and showed them kindness. Joseph yet had another opportunity to get revenge on his brothers after Jacob's death, but again he chose forgiveness.

Others, You, or God?

Anyone who has been deeply wronged knows that forgiveness like this does not come easily. How could Joseph choose forgiveness over vengeance? Joseph again experienced success because he held a proper perspective of God. Joseph did not view life in terms of what they did to him, but in terms of what God had done *through* him. He did not see time as "before my brothers were in control, but now I am in control." Rather, he viewed every moment of his life as completely under God's control. Joseph did not spit at his brothers, "You sold me!" Joseph told them, "God sent me!" Instead of seeing slavery, Joseph saw God's salvation. Because Joseph was there, he was able to interpret Pharaoh's dream. And because he was able to interpret Pharaoh's dream, he was able to save Egypt from famine. And because he was able to save Egypt from famine, his family had a place to go for food!

Joseph's Perspective

At the end of his life, Joseph did not describe his days as "few and evil," like his father Jacob did. No, Joseph said, *"God…hath made me forget all my toil and all my father's house"* (Genesis 41:51). The reason Joseph could say all of this was that he had the big-picture perspective. He perceived God as the Grand Writer of history, and he viewed his life as just one chapter in God's greater story. You see, Joseph's story wasn't about him. It wasn't even about his family. In fact, it wasn't even about the nation of Israel. Joseph's story was about God's story—and God's story was about the coming Messiah who would be born out of Joseph's family many years later. How epic is that! Joseph may not have fully realized that his family would produce a nation which would produce the Savior of the world— but he did realize that God was the Writer of a much grander story than his own. His perspective was one of gratitude that God would write his own life into the big picture.

Part of His Story

Let's consider our own perspectives. Is your life just your story? Or is it just a part of God's bigger, grander story? Like Joseph, we can experience success over self-pity, we can choose forgiveness over vengeance, when we have a proper perspective on God. The story is all about God, and like Joseph, we are just privileged to be a part of it!

Read

Romans 12:19

> Dearly beloved, avenge not yourselves, but rather give place unto wrath: for it is written, Vengeance is mine; I will repay, saith the Lord.

Romans 8:28

> And we know that all things work together for good to them that love God, to them who are the called according to his purpose.

Time to think!

HOW COULD JOSEPH CHOOSE FORGIVENESS OVER VENGEANCE?

_____

_____

_____

WHAT ARE SOME PARTS OF "YOUR STORY" THAT YOU NEED TO YIELD TO GOD (I.E. VENGEANCE)?

_____

_____

_____

Worth, Identity, and Purpose

In the pit, in the prison, and in the palace, Joseph *found his worth, identity, and purpose in God.* His brothers may have called him a slave, but Joseph knew he was a child of the King. His master may have treated him like a scoundrel, but Joseph knew he was saved by God's grace. His friends may have forgotten him, but Joseph rested in his purpose of giving good to others. Pharaoh may have praised his wisdom, but Joseph knew that all the praise belonged to God. At the end of his days, Joseph remembered a life of great purpose—not because it was his story, but because it had been God's story all along.